Japan's Transition to the Twenty-first Century

Number 4

Teikyo
Loretto
Heights
University

*Linking the Minds
of the World*

JAPAN STUDIES

Publications of the Center for Japan Studies at Teikyo Loretto Heights University

JAPAN'S TRANSITION TO THE 21st CENTURY

THE CENTER FOR JAPAN STUDIES

EDITED BY
SIDNEY DEVERE BROWN

A publication of the Center for Japan Studies at Teikyo Loretto Heights University, Denver, Colorado. Although the Center is responsible for the selection and acceptance of manuscripts in the series, responsibility for the opinions expressed and for the accuracy of statements rests with their authors.

Distributed by
Institute of East Asian Studies Publications
University of California
2223 Fulton St., MC#2318
Berkeley, California 94720-2318
E-mail: easia@uclink.berkeley.edu

Library of Congress Cataloging-in-Publication Data

Japan's transition to the twenty-first century / edited by Sidney DeVere Brown.
     p. cm. —.br
Comprising 8 essays selected from the papers presented at the Conference "Japan's
Transition to the Twenty-first Century", held October 4–6, 1998, in Denver, Colorado.
    Includes bibliographical references.
    ISBN 1-9650254-2-2 (alk. paper)
    1. Japan—Relations—Foreign
    countries—Congresses. 2. Japan—Civilization—
century—Congresses. I. Brown, Sidney D. II. Conference "Japan's Transition to the
Twenty-first Century" (1998 : Denver, Colo.)

DS885.48 .J37   2000
303.48'252'009049—dc21   00-060362

Contents

Contributors

Shoji Azuma is Associate Professor, Department of Languages and Literature, University of Utah.

Sawa Kurotani Becker is Assistant Professor of Anthropology at the University of Redlands.

Sidney DeVere Brown is Professor Emeritus of History at the University of Oklahoma and Regents Professor of History at the University of Science and Arts of Oklahoma.

Victoria Douglass is Assistant Professor in the AIHM Department at Oregon State University. The research for this work was done with support from the Japan Society for the Promotion of Science.

Kenichi Kamigaito is Professor of Comparative Culture, Tezuka-yama Gakuin University, Osaka, and the International Research Center for Japanese Studies, Kyoto.

Ronnie Littlejohn is Chair, Department of Philosophy, Belmont University, Nashville, Tennessee.

Kyoko Murakami is a Ph.D. candidate in the area of educational policy and leadership and currently is administrative assistant to the president at Josai International University, Tokyo.

Hiroko Storm is Associate Professor of Japan Studies, Teikyo Loretto Heights University, Denver, Colorado.

Introduction

SIDNEY DEVERE BROWN

"Japan's Transition to the Twenty-first Century" was the provocative theme of the conference that brought scholars together on the beautiful campus of Teikyo Loretto Heights University in Denver, Colorado, October 4–6, 1998, and eight of their timely papers are presented to the public in this small volume. All of the scholars have treated the basic theme in their own ways and identified significant changes in their special fields at the turn of the new century.

"Twenty-first century" is clearly a Western concept; it suggests that we are looking at Japan's relationship to the West and that Japan is virtually joining the Western comity of nations. Centuries are as likely to be used as era names, or *nengō*, for a summing up and a look to the future of Japan. A spate of studies of the Showa era (1926–89) accompanied the death of the Showa emperor in 1989, just as a new round of reflections on the past and speculations about the future is occasioned by the entry into the new millennium.

If anything, the Western chronology has a slight edge as a bench mark, even in Japan, which has retained its traditional year-periods for official dating when it might have gone over completely to the Western calendar. The first opportunity occurred on January 1, 1873, when the Western solar calendar was first adopted with its months and days, but the year remained Meiji 6. The other lost opportunity came on January 1, 1946, when the emperor declared his humanity (as the American occupiers expected), but kept the traditional chronology, Showa 21, for official use. Currently the popular practice seems to be moving toward the Western year system in spite of official practice, as *Asahi Shinbun*, the leading daily, gives the year as 1999 putting *Heisei 11 nen* in parentheses.

Bold predictions were once the order of the day among pundits on Japan. In 1970 Herman Kahn foresaw that the twenty-first century might belong to Japan, just as the nineteenth century was the era of Great Britain, and the twentieth century dominated by the United States of America. "It would not be surprising if the twenty-first century belonged to Japan," he wrote, and he could yet be right. But he clearly missed the mark in pinpointing 2000 as the target year for Japan "to surpass the most advanced Western countries in economic development."[1] Futurology has its limits. By contrast, currently gloom and doom prevail in hand-wringing about "the collapse of the bubble economy" or "the shadow of the miracle," surely just as far off the mark as the excessively optimistic predictions.

Contributors to this volume are more cautious than some of the famous pundits and have touched on the grand problems of economic growth, military security, and trade relations only obliquely, modestly seeking answers to smaller questions about Japan. Two of the papers use culture as the touchstone, examining Japan's relations with the East Asian continent and with the United States respectively.

Kenichi Kamigaito, the keynote speaker at the conference, recalls that classical Chinese was once the lingua franca of East Asia, but educational patterns diverged, and the very characters, the *kanji*, began to be written differently in China and Japan. When computers superseded calligraphy, different codes were adopted in the several polities, and communication by e-mail or Internet became an ordeal. What he proposes is a cultural rapprochement through an international conference to fashion a common computer code for ideographs to relink the nations of East Asia, which still retain an innate cultural familiarity toward one another.

Sidney D. Brown, the symposium speaker, likewise looks beyond geopolitical issues and trade friction to explore Japanese-American cultural relations through the careers of five people who have become practitioners or promoters of the culture of the other nation—a jazz musician, a collector of Japanese paintings, a translator of Japanese literature, a movie director, and a baseball player. They plus their enthusiastic and sometimes numerous fol-

---

[1] Herman Kahn, *The Emerging Japanese Superstate: Challenge and Response* (Englewood Cliffs, N.J.: Prentice-Hall, 1970), 2, 6.

lowers provide a vast unnoticed cultural link, the "glue" binding the two nations together.

Ronnie Littlejohn considers the several approaches to the study of moral culture and proposes the use of comparative pluralism, which gives value to differences as well as commonalities, suggesting that *amae*, which valorizes and anticipates the needs of others in Japan, would enrich the moral life of the United States.

Sawa Kurotani Becker has observed in studying corporate wives abroad that many are pulled away from traditional moral belief and practice. In theory, they are sent with their husbands to promote cultural reproduction in the home, protect the identity of family members in the domestic sphere, and provide a familiar "Japanese" domestic space for relaxation after work. Ironically, in practice, they sometimes live permanently in the United States with or without their husbands and undermine "the structure of power from the inside out."

Victoria Douglass has presented a very positive view of contemporary Japanese health care and implies that the United States has much to learn from it. Health care in Japan is more comprehensive than in any other country, and techniques for diagnosis and administration represent the wave of the future, from robotic care of infectious patients to automatic collection of linens in hospitals. In Japan, where it is not considered ethical to profit from the misfortunes of one's own people, health treatment is a caring rather than a money-making profession.

Kyoko Murakami, however, finds that Japan lags behind in sexual equality in the workforce, as one might expect, and that it perpetuates traditional ideas about gender roles in its textbooks. A latent content analysis of sixteen Japanese civics textbooks revealed that they undercut the intent of the Equal Employment Opportunity Law, reinforcing as they do traditional attitudes that women are responsible for household duties and that men are the breadwinners. The net result is that female students are discouraged from pursuing professional careers.

Other papers deal with the Japanese language in transition to the twenty-first century. Shoji Azuma has studied pseudo-borrowings, the treatment of Japanese words as if they were borrowed from abroad by writing them in *katakana*. "Modernity, sophistication, internationalization" are implied by this device, which is used for emphasis, distanced taboo, negative politeness, and other purposes. The Japanese language continues to evolve as the twenty-first century arrives, and influences have washed in from the West.

Hiroko Storm has identified changes in spoken Japanese, with deaccentuation of longer words among native speakers of the Tokyo dialect, the national language. Since English is heavily accented, and accents carry over into the Japanese as learned by English speakers in the classroom, the gap between native speakers and foreign-student speakers of Japanese is widening, and pedagogues should take heed.

Those who gathered at Teikyo Loretto Heights University to discuss Japan's transition to the twenty-first century tended toward optimism rather than alarm. Neither China nor the United States seemed particularly threatening, and exploration of the cultural dimension generally revealed broad rapport between Japan and those countries. Although Japan is caught up in globalization, and Western values continue to arrive through the medium of corporate wives and other avenues, Japan has its own contributions to make—in medicine as a caring industry and in moral culture through greater concerns for the needs of others. Acculturation, silent change, may in the long run play as important a role as the great national economic and security problems in shaping Japan's twenty-first century.

ONE

Japan's Relationship to East Asia in the Twenty-first Century

KENICHI KAMIGAITO

Some people say that the twenty-first century will be the century of East Asia. This observation derives from the remarkable economic growth in several East Asian countries, such as mainland China, Korea, and Taiwan, in recent years. In spite of the economic recession in Southeast and East Asia during 1998, the long-term prognosis is that a high growth rate will prevail in East Asia, compared to other areas, for several decades to come.

Recently I lectured to Korean students on the Korean-Japanese relationship in premodern times, and, unexpectedly, their response to my topic was rather future-oriented. One of the Korean students asked me if it is possible for Japan and Korea to build an economic community such as the developing European community (EC). My reply was pessimistic. Japan has little or no chance of forming a community such as the EC in East Asia because the political environment around Japan has been far more hostile than in Western Europe after 1945, where there was a strong will between the two major countries, Germany and France, to cancel their hatred and to promote friendship and trust. By contrast, the Japanese government has been reluctant to apologize for its exploitative colonization of Korea and has virtually ignored the great damage the Japanese army did in China during the Second World War. Both countries remain alienated.

During the era of American dominance in East Asia after 1945, Japan paid little attention to China and Korea, whose economic and political strength were negligible. I believe that it was a mistake for Japan to overlook the potential power, and strong will, of the East Asian countries to develop themselves and to be inconsiderate of the feelings of the Chinese and Korean people. The Korean economy after the 1970s, and the Chinese economy after the 1980s, experienced unprecedented growth; consequently, Japanese premiers and emperors began to apologize for past misdeeds to ingratiate themselves, as they visited those countries and invited the top leaders of the two countries to Japan. But their words of regret appeared to be reluctant, and Ministry of Foreign Affairs officials usually bargained sharply over the exact wording of the apology in preliminary negotiations. In fact, Japan appears to have barred the door to the East Asian community by allowing those people to remain skeptical that the Great East Asia Co-prosperity Sphere is entirely dead. One great obstacle to the establishment of an East Asian community is that several of the countries, such as mainland China and North Korea, are not democratic at all. Japan cannot consider such countries as reliable partners even if they are "brothers" by reason of culture and history. For Japan, the United States is a far more reliable partner, even if it is not a blood brother in cultural terms.

An outstanding Chinese poet, thinker, and diplomat, Huang Zunxian (1848–1905) in his writings stressed the unity of the East Asian people who belong to the same race and share a common system of writing (*tongzhong tongwen*). Racially the Japanese derived mainly from South China, as did rice cultivation, having entered by way of South Korea and Kyushu. Writing followed a similar path, as did Chinese literature, the Chinese word *wen* standing both for the letters and literature; and Huang communicated quite freely with Japanese intellectuals in the 1880s in written Chinese, *kanbun* to the Japanese, in so-called brush speech (J. *hitsudan;* C. *bitan*). For him and his Japanese friends, written classical Chinese was clearly the lingua franca of East Asia. Indeed, the Japanese foreign minister of the 1870s, Soejima Taneomi (1828–1905), could boast of a poetic ability in classical Chinese on a par with that of Chinese ministers.

The 1880s was the last period of classical Chinese as the universal language of East Asian intellectuals; the next generation of Japanese learned Western languages as their first foreign language. Then, China's new generation also started to abandon classical education. Typically, the new Chinese political leader, Sun Yat-sen, could read and write English freely, but his knowledge of the Chinese classics was limited. He talked with Japanese comrades in English or through interpreters, not by *bitan*.

In Japan after the Sino-Japanese War of 1894–95, the Chinese language was neglected under the influence of the nationalistic education of the times. In mainland China after 1949 education in the Chinese classics was abandoned altogether; and in Korea after 1945, although Confucian ethics survived, even less attention was devoted to the Chinese classics in high school than in Japan. Classical Chinese, consequently, ceased to be the lingua franca of East Asia. Still, Chinese characters were central to language education in mainland China, Taiwan, Japan, and to a certain degree in South Korea. In North Korea, however, Chinese characters were abolished completely. I once met a North Korean youth in a compartment of an international train en route from Ulan Bator to Beijing, and we talked in Korean a great deal for two days. Just before we arrived in Beijing he wrote his name and address in *hangul*, asking me to call him if I should visit Pyongyang. When I asked him in which Chinese characters his name would be written, his reply surprised me: he said that he did not know the characters for his own name. South Korea and Taiwan are still using the traditional characters; mainland China is using characters, but in greatly simplified form, the *jiantizi*. Japan has simplified them, but not so radically as China. In mainland China, Japan, and South Korea, therefore, Chinese characters have survived, but all three countries are using different forms. The unity of written language that Huang Zunxian found in the 1880s has been lost. Yet, simplified though they are, they still have their origin in the old Chinese characters and look very much alike. It is not so difficult for a Japanese to identify familiar characters in the abbreviated writing of the People's Republic of China.

Japanese foods are quite different from the cuisine of China, and yet they have some elements in common such as soy sauce and miso. When traveling in the West, Japanese tourists usually seek out Chinese restaurants in cities too small to have Japanese restaurants, as Chinese food is more familiar than Western food to them. Likewise, for Japanese the Chinese language is more familiar than the alphabetic languages of the West, because the Chinese characters are known to them. I lived in Edmonton, Canada, in 1994 with my wife and five-year-old daughter. It is a provincial city, not to be compared with the largest North American cities, but still it is modern, having the best urban facilities, big malls, supermarkets, swimming pools, efficient medical service, everything. We truly enjoyed living in this Canadian city, as all the people were friendly to us, and the democratic social system was impressive. Compare this, then, to Beijing where we lived for five months in 1993. Because I was teaching in a graduate school, we lived in an apartment of a big national hotel for foreign experts. Although it must have been the most comfortable life in Beijing, I experienced innumerable inconveniences in shopping, transportation, and medical service; and the political system is not at all democratic. In spite of all that I felt immeasurable empathy with the Chinese people and the Chinese way of life. The feeling was more than simple racial sympathy. In Canada I encountered some native peoples, and felt sympathy for them in their oppression, but not so deep a feeling as I experienced for the Chinese people. Racially, Native Americans, Chinese, and Japanese belong to the same Mongoloid group; but culturally we Japanese incline toward China because its influence pervaded our land from the third century B.C. to the nineteenth century. Unconsciously we feel a kinship for the Chinese without being able to explain why. At present, Japanese youth are beginning to identify with America in the cultural sense, as they have so many things in common—McDonald's hamburgers, Coca-Cola, baseball, and democracy, to name a few. Although these things are important, they are not deep-rooted, and even the youngest Japanese may feel closer to China if they have lived in both China and the United States.

Taking this feeling for Chinese culture into account, the seemingly firm Japanese-American alliance may not be so stable after all. Moreover, in the twenty-first century just ahead, the Chinese economy will probably develop faster than its American counterpart, even though interrupted by the inevitable political disturbances, and become a more significant link to Japan. Beyond that more and more Chinese people are immigrating into Japan, and the rate of increase of Chinese restaurants in Japan suggests a growing taste in our land for Chinese foods. My concern is the significance of such "cultural familiarity" in building a good Sino-Japanese relationship in the course of the twenty-first century. English—not Japanese, not Chinese, not Korean—is being learned most eagerly as the first foreign language throughout East Asia. The only hopeful sign for unity is that Chinese has passed up German as the second foreign language in Japan and Korea, and might serve as a bond. But is that enough to reestablish the East Asian community?

If the historic cultural unity of East Asia, based on common usage of Chinese characters, is to reemerge, certain problems must be resolved. One difficulty centers on the divergence of writing systems: Chinese characters differ in the written languages of Japan, China, and South Korea; in North Korea and Vietnam, they have been abolished altogether. Further, different computer codes have been developed to identify the same Chinese characters in different countries. Confusion among the so-called double-byte codes has created an electronic Babel. Using the Japanese operating system, it is difficult to read e-mail from mainland China or Taiwan or to show Chinese characters on the home pages of China, which are written in GB (mainland), or Big 5 (Hong Kong, Taiwan) codes. As a result of the independent development of a policy for encoding Chinese characters by each government, not only do the forms of the same Chinese characters differ, but the codes differ as well. If the political unity of the East Asian community had been a reality, representatives of the various East Asian nations would surely have discussed and created a single code for Chinese characters. Because of the absurd confusion in using Chinese characters on our computers, a conference needs to be held to devise a new method for handling them. The problem reaches even into the diverse language educational systems throughout the region and can be resolved only by the governments themselves (although a conference of knowledgeable individuals might hasten the solution). Ten years ago, when we worked at our computers in isolation from other areas of the world, we were not concerned by this problem. But now every computer is connected to the World Wide Web, and East Asia's people, in particular, need to speak each other's language and to decode computerized mail, home pages, and databases. When Japan and China decided on their respective new simplified characters, there was no diplomatic relationship between the two countries. Japan's revised characters were released to the public in 1949, the very year of the foundation of the People's Republic of China, which was then in isolation from Japan and the West. China's simplified characters were announced in 1956, long before normalization of diplomatic relations between Japan and China took place in 1972. The two simplified character systems were formed separately, therefore, without any discussion or negotiation between the interested parties. In Taiwan, in contrast, the Nationalist government has maintained the traditional characters. The so-called *fangti*, or complicated characters, are inconvenient for writing colloquial Chinese. On the other hand, they are far more useful for writing and printing the Chinese classics than are the simplified characters. In Japan, the Chinese classics are printed in traditional characters; in mainland China they used to be done in simplified characters, but more recently they have often been published in the older traditional characters. Probably this shift corresponds to the reevaluation of traditional culture, including Confucianism, on the mainland. In Taiwan, Confucian philosophy is orthodox; and it is a principle of national education to maintain tradition, including the old, complicated characters. Taiwan is the most conservative, or the most sophisticated, of the countries in its usage of Chinese characters in computers. Its Big 5 code contains twice as many characters, about 13,000, as do those of Japan or of mainland China, which have about 7,000 each. If one intends to construct a database of the Chinese classics, the Taiwanese code (Big 5) is far better than those of Japan and mainland China.

I access the Chinese classics database of Academia Sinica in Taiwan, via the Internet, almost daily, and feel that this is the greatest database of literature in East Asia. It includes almost all of the basic Chinese classics and all of the dynastic histories as well. Building such a database of the classics in Japan and mainland China would be inconvenient because it would require so many characters not normally used. If you are writing with a computer, it makes no difference whether you choose the simplified or the complicated fonts. In mainland China, more and more people are writing with computers, and some day such writers may become the majority. The old, complicated characters may come to life again, along with the revival of traditional culture; and there will be no reason to insist on educating the laboring class with the ugly simplified writing systems once all people are able to write with their computers.

I visited Mongolia in 1988 when Mongolian was written with the Russian alphabet. A Mongolian expert at the Japanese embassy in Ulan Bator explained to me that there is a Mongolian alphabet and that it is a very efficient writing system, but it was very difficult for Mongolia to abolish the Russian alphabet and restore the traditional Mongolian writing. To change the national writing system is a major undertaking. Yet sometimes nationalistic passion overcomes all obstacles; and two years after my conversation with the above-mentioned expert, the Mongolian alphabet became once again the official writing system for the Mongolian nation. Chinese simplified characters, however, are still Chinese characters; they were not forced on the country by pro-Moscow politicians as was the case with the Russian alphabet in Mongolia. But what has occurred in Mongolia, with a comeback of the traditional characters, may happen in mainland China also.

North Korea has banished the Chinese characters from elementary education, but, considering that China is North Korea's only ally, would it not be better for North Korea to revive education in Chinese characters? In the 1950s, the Communist Party in mainland China intended to make the roman alphabet the official writing system, but the plan was given up very quickly. In the twenty-first century Chinese characters will surely continue to be the national writing system there. In Japan early in the 1980s there was a movement to abolish the use of Chinese characters because they could not be accommodated on the poor computers of the era; but today Japanese are writing Chinese characters easily on their computers, and they complain only that the present JIS code does not include enough of them. Microsoft is intending to make its so-called unicode the world's universal letter code system. But is it proper to let a private company decide how Chinese characters will be encoded in a computer operating system? Because Microsoft has monopolized the operating system market, at present its unicode is the only solution to the problem of uniting the divided character codes of East Asia. The writing of Chinese characters with computers, however, is now of concern to all East Asian people. Should not the decision on which characters are to be taken into the new universal code be decided by an East Asian conference that includes members of national language councils, ministries of education, representatives of PEN clubs, poets, writers, journalists, and computer software engineers? It would be a real Babel, because there are so many arguments inside each nation concerning Chinese character education and the usage of Chinese characters itself. Already an enormous volume of information is being exchanged between Japan and the other East Asian countries in Chinese characters, and everyone complains of the inconvenience caused by different codes. Japan as the leading country in Asia in technology should take the responsibility for organizing a conference to establish a genuine universal code system. At the conference Japan should not compel the adoption of its own code system, but allow equality among the participants. As complicated as the Chinese character problem is, political unification will be even more difficult.

I have taken Chinese characters as an example of how deep is the cultural relationship among the East Asian countries and of the complications flowing from the disintegration of the writing system. For Japan in the twenty-first century the relationship with East Asian countries will be crucial, as important as its relationship across the Pacific with the United States. The Chinese diplomat Huang Zunxian lived in both Japan and the United States, and afterward he concluded that China, Korea, and Japan should form a league with America as an ally because it was the least aggressive of the Western nations (*Zhaoxiancaolue* [On Korean diplomatic policy], 1881). This scheme still has validity, even though the most dangerous potential enemy of that era, Russia, has apparently lost its power. The geopolitical location of Japan is the same in the twenty-first century as before. The United States and China are still the most important countries for Japan. When the American fleet of Matthew C. Perry visited Japan in 1853, Western culture and American democracy were totally alien to the Japanese people.

I was born in 1948, and speak poor English, because it was very difficult for members of our generation to leave the country to live in an English-speaking nation. I hope that Japan is conducting Western democracy better than I speak English. To me, Chinese characters and foods cooked with soya sauce are more familiar than English and McDonald's hamburgers; but I do hope that Japanese of the next generation will be exposed to the two cultures equally and be in harmony with both. My daughter lived for half a year in Beijing when she was two years old, and she spoke the Beijing dialect perfectly. She has forgotten all of her Chinese now, but some day, when she studies in China, her ability in that language will revive, I hope. She went to kindergarten in Edmonton, Canada, for two semesters when she was five. Some day, when she studies in an American university, she will acquire a perfect accent in English. Japan's relationship with East Asia should not be an updated version of the Greater East Asia Co-Prosperity Sphere, which took the United States as its adversary, Japan alone dominating. Geopolitically, the Japanese Archipelago is situated between America and China, being somewhat closer to China, but the three nations are like stepping-stones. Technological progress in transportation and communication has shrunk the distance across the Pacific; and Japanese youth of the twenty-first century should be enabled to observe the cultures of both America and China more closely, and more impartially, than I. But if they know only the taste of American beef and ignore the taste of the great traditional Chinese foods, I shall be disappointed. Forgetting not East Asia, while becoming friendly with America, is the path Japan should take in the twenty-first century.

TWO

The Future of Japanese-American Cultural Relations

SIDNEY DEVERE BROWN

This chapter should be labeled a study of the law of unintended consequences. My experience at the Navy Oriental Languages School in Boulder, Colorado, during World War II is a nice illustration of the point. We spent fourteen months in an intensive course in Japanese to prepare to win the war in the Pacific, yet, for many of us, the interesting and demanding work was preparation for careers in Japanese studies at universities in the United States. Few of those in my class faced the enemy under fire, but nearly all of us came to know Japanese culture, to admire our *sensei* of Japanese descent, and to become Japanophiles for the rest of our lives.

In the postwar years the law of unintended consequences worked itself out as officials of the two nations focused on the great issues of security and trade, but ordinary citizens became entranced with some aspect or another of the culture of the opposite nation. The defensive alliance embodied in the security treaty of 1952 brought millions of American servicemen to Japan, and, while many could not have cared less about Japanese culture, others stayed around, and they or their wives became experts on Japanese pottery, bonsai, ikebana, judo, or any number of unique features of that land's society. Trans-Pacific trade likewise brought the two nations together, as Japan first sought to balance its accounts in the 1950s, then the United States became frantic over its unprecedented unfavorable balance in the 1970s. The significance for this chapter is that economic forces moved so many who were intrigued with the other's culture across the ocean.

Two splendid books on Japanese-American relations, based on careful documentary research and written with style, appeared in 1997: Walter LaFeber, *The Clash: U.S.-Japanese Relations throughout*

History (New York: Norton, 1997), and Michael Schaller, *Altered States: The United States and Japan since the Occupation* (Oxford: Oxford University Press, 1997). In dealing with the formal aspects of diplomatic relations, they provide analyses of almost continuous quarrels and their resolution and leave us with an impression of leaders of the two nations glowering at one another across the Pacific.

Cultural relations, which are less visible and less dramatic, are generally omitted from such studies. My purpose here is to explore the cultural strands that link Japan and the United States, a subject that could begin with influences on daily life (e.g., sushi and MacDonald's hamburgers) and extend across the board. I shall confine myself, however, to five case studies of important people who have been attracted to the other nation's culture, each creating a strand in the invisible bond that ties the nations together. The focus will be on a jazz musician, a collector of traditional Japanese painting, a translator and critic of Japanese literature, a film director, and a baseball player.

Leaders in Intercultural Relations

Oda Satoru

Jazz is one significant cultural link across the Pacific, and Oda Satoru (b. 1927), tenor saxophonist, typifies the vigor of the relationship. His quartet draws capacity crowds to Swing City in the Ginza, Tokyo, and other venues; and he demonstrated that he is a world-class musician by "breaking it up" at the Monterey Jazz Festival on this side of the Pacific in 1985 with his inventive solo on "Just Friends." Afterward, Oda played in that world-renowned festival nine more times.

Jazz, America's most important original art form, was introduced to Japan in the 1920s via orchestras aboard trans-Pacific passenger liners, went into the dance halls of Yokohama and Kobe, and spread throughout the land with the popularity of the phonograph record. The pioneer recording of "My Blue Heaven" with Japanese lyrics as "Aozora" by Japan Columbia sold 250,000 copies in 1928.

In the 1930s, however, during the era of National Spiritual Mobilization, when Satoru had his schooling, jazz was denounced as a symbol of American decadence. Western music was acceptable only as long as its harmonies were used for martial music and other patriotic purposes. The splendid public school music program (of American origin), in place since 1878, enabled him to enter the Imperial Navy Band school at Yokosuka as one of a hundred students selected in nationwide competition in 1943. There he underwent rigorous training on the tenor saxophone, learned several new scores each week, and was a member of the band that was placed aboard the giant aircraft carrier *Shinano* in 1945, only to be pulled off just before the ship left for Okinawa, where it went down with all hands.[1]

Demobilized at the end of the lost war, he made his discouraging way to his home through Nagoya, Osaka, and Hiroshima, ruined by American air raids, to his native Kyushu. His next older brother (in a family of ten) had been killed in the naval war with the Americans, and Satoru was vexed by the sight of kimono-clad Japanese girls on the arms of American soldiers with the Occupation forces. But Satoru did have to live, and his network of navy musicians led him to play with a band at the American Officers Club in Hakata, Fukuoka. By day he listened to the jukebox at the club and tried to discern the technique for ad lib solos by famous players.

By 1947 Satoru was in Tokyo, riding the bus nightly to play at the American clubs at Tachikawa Air Force Base on the western outskirts of the city and other places, building a reputation; and when social dancing became a craze among the Japanese people liberated from the strictures of wartime, he found jobs enough playing for Japanese dancers, then for Japanese listeners to small-group jazz, principally university students, in the cabarets on the Ginza, when jazz became a craze about 1952–53. He joined the most popular of these combos, the Gay Septet of Raymond Conde, Filipino-born clarinetist, and was soon called "the Japanese Lester Young" by a friendly critic.[2] Satoru does belong to the Lester

---

[1] Oda Satoru, *Sake to Bara no Hibi: Ore no Jyazzu Jinsei 50 Nen* (Days of wine and roses: My jazz life of fifty years) (Tokyo: F. A. Shuppan, 1993), 109–110.

[2] At Birdland, Roppongi, Tokyo, in 1983, Mundell Lowe, the visiting jazz guitarist who was in the audience, requested "Tickle Toe," a Lester Young classic, and Satoru returned after intermission to render a stirring rendition of it.

Satoru plays standards in his distinctive style—light tone, long, flowing lines. At Cytheria, a Ginza, Tokyo, jazz club, on June 30, 1987, he opened a set with "Lady Be Good," a Lester Young classic, and continued with "Round Midnight," "Sweet Lorraine," and "Someday Sweetheart," a 1920s Chicago jazz number.

At Swing City, Ginza, on May 29, 1998, he played "Sweet Georgia Brown" with his quartet (on seeing me, as it is a favorite of mine), then did "In a Sentimental Mood," an Ellington number; "South of the Border," "Moonlight in Vermont," "You Belong to Me" (for request time), "These Foolish Things," "Things Ain't

Young school of tenor saxophonists, as do Zoot Sims, Stan Getz, and Paul Quinichette, but he has his own originality, which has been recognized by visiting American jazzmen. It was Hank Jones, pianist, at Monterey in 1985, who took Satoru under his wing, helping him to overcome his aversion to America and Americans, inherited from the war. They made several records together.

Satoru played Kansas City–style jazz in Tokyo, and at Monterey he played with Jay McShann, Kansas City pianist, whose rhythm section made the Japanese jazzman "ecstatic." "That rhythm. I was amidst the rhythm I love, a feeling not to be described by tongue or pen."[3] Satoru, five-foot two, played for five hours, alternating with Buddy Tate, a tenor saxophonist six and a half feet tall. Musically, however, they were on the same wave length.

Akiyoshi Toshiko, a sixteen-year-old refugee from Manchuria and classical pianist when Satoru first met her in Kyushu, came to Tokyo to join him in 1947 and ultimately mastered the Bud Powell style of bebop piano. She then migrated to the United States, where she has sought not to perpetuate the received tradition, as has Satoru,[4] but to incorporate Japanese musical elements into the arrangements for her big band, which performed weekly at Birdland on 44th Street in New York in 1998. The two are a few of the Japanese jazz artists who in their different ways have won the respect of American musicians and become part of the international jazz world. With their fans, the Japanese jazz critics, and jazz historians, they have kept alive and developed further an American music that has its own devoted following in Japan. *Swing Journal*, their organ, publishes a 400-page monthly slick magazine that dwarfs any American jazz journal for size and circulation.

What They Used to Be," another Ellington composition; "Avalon," "Stardust," "It's a Sin to Tell a Lie," which brought loud applause on being identified; "I've Got You Under My Skin," and "Moten Swing," a closer out of the Kansas City repertoire.

[3] Oda, *Sake to Bara no Hibi*, 109–10.

[4] When Hank Jones told Satoru that he should make use of his "yellow roots," he began to practice on the *shakuhachi*, the Japanese recorder, but he has not brought that element into his music. Interestingly, his wife, Junko, was in her youth a Japanese classical dancer performing at the Embujo in Shimbashi, and their granddaughter is a student at the Peers University studying traditional theater and music. So the family mixes East and West without difficulty. Interview with Oda Satoru, Tokyo, May 30, 1998, Tokyo.

Joe Price

Among the arts, painting joins West and East as strongly as any of the forms, and Joe Price, formerly of Bartlesville, Oklahoma, is the leading collector of Edo-period (1600–1850) art in the Western world. He has become a major force in joining the art worlds of Japan and America.

When Japanese painters were drawn to Paris and began painting in oils after the manner of the French impressionists, traditional Japanese painting was regarded in its own land as inferior, hardly worth preserving. Ernest Fenollosa, a visiting professor of political economy at the new Tokyo Imperial University in the 1870s, who assembled the great collection of Japanese painting for the Boston Museum of Fine Arts, is often given credit for having restored pride in the native painting tradition.

Joe Price is a contemporary counterpart of Fenollosa. He retired a multimillionaire from the presidency of the family pipeline firm at the age of fifty-three to spend the rest of his life collecting and exhibiting the art for which he has a great love, a love so great that Price once broke into tears on viewing an Itō Jakuchū (1716–1800) masterpiece at the Imperial palace in Kyoto, writes a Japanese art historian who was an eyewitness.[5] He has assembled his own remarkable collection of four hundred screens and scrolls from the Edo period.

How did an Oklahoma engineer develop such passion for an exotic art form? The question cannot be answered easily. Price himself remembers that he bought his first Edo painting at a gallery on Madison Avenue in New York in 1953 without knowing anything about the artist. The price was very low. He simply admired the work, and the style grew on him. Bruce Goff, an architecture dean at the University of Oklahoma, was one influence on his student Price: Goff sometimes played traditional Gagaku court music for his Oklahoma students, and he preached the Japan-influenced design gospel of Frank Lloyd Wright. Both Goff and Wright were devotees of woodblock prints, and Joe Price had direct contact with Frank Lloyd Wright when the great architect was retained to build the nineteen-story Price tower in Bartlesville and to design a home for a family member on the large Price estate.

---

[5] Yūzō Yamane, "Joe Price and the Shin'enkan Collection," in *Masterpieces from the Shin'enkan Collection: Japanese Painting of the Edo Period*, trans. Robert T. Singer 8–9 (Los Angeles: Los Angeles County Museum of Art, 1986).

By 1963 Price had made his first trip to Japan. He began his
collection on the basis of intuition, but subsequently he relied on
his Japanese wife, Etsuko, to assist in the development of the collection, which featured six-fold screens and hanging scrolls of the
great individualist Itō Jakuchū, as well as others of the Rimpa
school (e.g., Sakai Hōitsu). For a man who had spent much of his
adult life building pipelines in lonely places in the desert or
beyond the Arctic Circle, the life of a collector of Japanese art had
its appeal.[6]

Price built his Shin'enkan mansion, a residence and art gallery
designed by Bruce Goff, to show off his collection, using no more
light than the natural rays of the "delicately changing light of the
sun," as was done in castles of the Edo era. A reflecting pool of
water in the main gallery kept humidity at the desired level and
enhanced the beauty of Hōitsu's painting on gold-leaf of thirty-six
poets shown to me by Price himself, after he put away the fierce
and dangerous watchdog that guarded his invaluable collection
and admitted me to the grounds near Bartlesville.

Price has used his wealth to make the collection more accessible. It has been shown at the Sony Museum in Tokyo, at the Dal-
las Museum of Art, in the meantime, and before that in part at the
Tokyo National Museum. Later Price arranged to have the collection exhibited at the Los Angeles Museum of Art in an appropriate building also designed by Goff. Mr. and Mrs. Price now maintain residences in both Roppongi, Tokyo, and Corona del Mar,
California,[7] and have become major figures in the art worlds of the
two lands. Japanese painting gains devotees in the United States
with each showing of these magnificent six-fold screens and paintings. Viewers develop appreciation for the linear style of painting
and see the works not as mere cartoons, with awkward perspective, but as splendid works of art that have moved Japanese
viewers for centuries.

---

[6] Ibid., 8–12.

[7] When the Prices left Oklahoma they donated their Shin'enkan mansion to the
University of Oklahoma for occasional conferences, but unfortunately in 1998 it
burned to the ground in an unexplained fire. Beautiful as it was the house was not
fireproof; fortunately, the great collection had long since been moved elsewhere.

Donald B. Keene

Japanese literature was less well known than Japanese painting in the United States before World War II, but in the half century since that conflict it has entered the mainstream. Because of the elegant translations of Donald B. Keene (b. 1922) and a few others, it is reviewed regularly in the *New York Times Book Review*. Most of the best translators were graduates of the Navy Oriental Languages School in Boulder. These included not only Keene, but also Edward Seidensticker, a native son of Colorado from Castle Rock, and Ivan Morris, who was in the U.S. Navy but spoke with a British accent and rode around the sleepy town of Boulder in 1944 in a sixteen-cylinder Dusenberg. Morris's affluence derived from the Chicago meat-packing fortune of his grandfather Ira Nelson Morris.

That trio—Keene, Seidensticker, and Morris—made the classic works of Japanese literature, ancient and modern, available to the American public in eminently readable form. The truly heroic figure among them was Donald Keene of Brooklyn, New York. On navy duty in the Pacific Keene read Japanese diaries as part of his work and developed a grudging admiration for the writers' "consecration... to their cause" as opposed to the "total indifference of most Americans to anything except returning home."[8] In fact, the Boulder language school contributed more in peace than in war. Among other things it enabled Keene to finish the agenda laid down by his great *sensei* at Columbia University, Tsunoda Ryūsaku, to write not only about the eighteenth-century iconoclast Honda Toshiaki, to whom Tsunoda introduced him, but to translate the puppet-theater dramas of Chikamatsu and the classic repertoire of the Noh theater. It also led him to write his magnum opus, a four-volume history of Japanese literature, over which he labored for twenty-seven years while teaching at Columbia. His limpid prose is a joy to read, and his knowledge of the subject is awesome. At the end of his career Keene became a guest columnist for Japan's greatest newspaper, the *Asahi Shimbun*, and for ten years, from 1982 to 1992, he contributed a daily column on Japanese diaries or on Japanese writers he had known. The name of Donald Keene became very nearly the best known of any American in Japan.

---

[8] Donald Keene, *On Familiar Terms: A Journey across Cultures* (New York/Tokyo: Kodansha International, 1994), 23.

A compulsive writer, Keene has confessed that he becomes nervous after a few days away from the typewriter. His enthusiasm for his field is admirable. His satisfaction at being the first to read almost any Japanese book he laid his hands on in the Columbia University library carried him through any self-doubt about his chosen field. Early in his career he was bemused by queries about his exotic specialty—"Why did you take that up?"—and in making his journey across cultures he assumed a modest, self-effacing persona, but surely he took pride in the recognition that has come to him in both Japan and the United States.

Keene is less well known in the United States than in Japan, but his influence is pervasive. The author of fifty-three books and translations, he has made the great Japanese literary classics generally available. Generations of students in my Japanese history classes have read *Chūshingura*, the kabuki play on the forty-seven loyal ronin, and *Essays in Idleness*, the miscellany highlighting Japanese aesthetics, using Keene's superb translations.

Seidensticker was the translator who made Kawabata Yasunari famous. The Nobel Prize Committee, who read works only in English or French, relied on his excellent English versions of *Snow Country* and *A Thousand Cranes*. In reward Seidensticker was invited in 1968 to accompany Kawabata to Stockholm as his interpreter at the prize ceremony; he acquired his first tuxedo for the occasion. Seidensticker also produced a new translation of *The Tale of Genji*.

The late Ivan Morris is remembered for *The Pillow Book of Lady Sei Shōnagon* and for Mishima's *Temple of the Golden Pavilion*. Ivan was my exact contemporary, and when we were young men working together at the Navy Department, I sometimes went to Chinese restaurants with him for lunch or drank tea with him during the afternoon break. His brilliant conversation from the year that we were both twenty-one remains in my mind still.

American literature, in its turn, has influenced Japanese writers, as Ōe Kenzaburo, the second Japanese writer to win the Nobel Prize in literature, reminds us. He read *Huckleberry Finn* at the American Cultural Center in Takamatsu day by day as a youth (he could not check it out), and *The Silent Cry* gives some evidence of the influence of Mark Twain's classic. From an early day Japan was the recipient of Western literature in translated form. To reverse the cultural flow was the great achievement of Keene, Seidensticker, and Morris.

Akira Kurosawa

Japanese film has had a greater influence on America, and on the world, than Japanese literature. Kurosawa Akira (1910–98) is a name universally known among film buffs in the United States. His *New York Times* obituary was longer than that of any American in recent memory, attesting to his importance here.

Initially, the flow of film influences was westward out of Hollywood. Japanese audiences flocked to the theater to see American movies even in the dark days of militarist Japan in the 1930s. Charlie Chaplin was a celebrity by the time he stepped off a trans-Pacific passenger vessel in Yokohama in 1931. Segawa Masahisa, banker and jazz historian, remembers that he and his classmates at the Peers School saw all of the Bing Crosby movies, such as *Waikiki Wedding,* and talked about them constantly.

To improve our comprehension of the spoken language, we students of the Navy Oriental Languages School in Boulder were shown a feature film in Japanese every Wednesday night. In fact, we understood little, but we saw enough to develop a negative view of the Japanese prewar film—comics in the pie-throwing era (perhaps Enomoto Ken'ichi made them), overly dramatic productions in which the distraught hero teetered on the edge of a cliff as he contemplated leaping into the sea (to the accompaniment of "Old Folks at Home" on the sound track), and handsome, sinister, mustachioed Americanized villains who wore stylish hats and leather jackets, not the native kimono.

Kurosawa's emergence on the world in 1950 with *Rashomon* brought a different, sophisticated Japanese film to American attention, winning the Academy Award for best foreign film in that year. *Rashomon* had a theme—that truth is elusive, that people "cannot survive without lies to make them feel they are better people than they really are." The bandit, the noblewoman, the ghost of the slain husband, and the woodcutter each told the story differently. "Human beings are unable to be honest with themselves about themselves. They cannot talk about themselves without embellishing," Kurosawa explained.[9] The film is based on two short stories by Akutagawa Ryunosuke (1892–1927), stories first translated into English by Glenn Shaw, civilian director of the Navy Oriental Languages School at the University of Colorado.

---

[9] Akira Kurosawa, *Something like an Autobiography,* trans. Audie E. Bock (New York: Alfred A. Knopf, 1982), 183.

Shaw had translated them in his days as a Kobe newspaperman before the war.

Throne of Blood, drawn from Shakespeare's *Macbeth*, was shown during the Shakespeare 400th anniversary celebration on the Boulder campus, while I was teaching summer school there. Its dramatic finale, with the tragic lord (played by Mifune Toshirō) standing in a burning castle as real arrows pinned him to the post, is unforgettable. Clearly, Kurosawa had developed and mastered a new style of cinema, in composition, movement, and all of the elements that enthrall the eye.[10]

No Regrets for our Youth (1946) has a message: the need for academic freedom from the right-wing elements that were in control in the 1930s. *Ikiru* (1952), in which a bureaucrat dying of cancer helps slum parents build a playground, is my favorite. *Seven Samurai* (1954) was a great action film; it inspired an American adaptation, *The Magnificent Seven*, reversing the usual flow of ideas.

Inasmuch as Kurosawa himself seldom traveled to the United States, it might have been more in keeping with my approach so far to have told about Donald Richie or Audie Bock as proselyters for Japanese cinema in this country. I have gone to the man himself, however, because his films and ideas have circulated the length and breadth of the land and shaped our images of Japan. I own sixteen of his videos with subtitles, and several more are available in this country, demonstrating the grip of his movies here.

Oh Sadaharu

Unlike the movies, which might have filtered into Japan from Paris as much as from Hollywood, baseball is clearly an American game. But there are Japanese heroes who have nurtured the game into the great national sport, in Japan as much as in the United States. Oh Sadaharu (b. 1940), the all-time great home-run hitter for the Yomiuri Giants, with his eight hundred plus home runs, did for the game in Japan what Mark McGuire did with his seventy in the summer of 1998 in the United States.

---

[10] Ibid., passim; Rich Lyman, "Akira Kurosawa, Director of Epics, Dies at 88," *New York Times*, September 7, 1998, A1, A12; "Akira Kurosawa," *The Economist*, September 12, 1998, 100.

Baseball was imported to Japan in the 1870s. One tradition is that Horace Wilson, an American who taught at the forerunner of Tokyo University, formed the first team in 1873. A photograph of this team at the Japanese Baseball Hall of Fame at Korakuen Stadium shows Makino Nobuaki on second base. Undoubtedly the future foreign minister, son of the great Meiji leader Ōkubo Toshimichi, learned the rudiments of the game during his stay as a student at a Quaker school in Philadelphia. Kido Takayoshi was said to have brought a baseball home when he returned from the Iwakura Mission to America and Europe in 1873 and to have had a shoemaker attempt to duplicate it when the ball wore out from excessive use by neighborhood boys.

The game developed in Japan with the abolition of the samurai class in the 1870s when young Japanese men were looking for a new competitive sport to replace kendō and the other martial arts so closely related to the military role of their former class. Baseball was the perfect replacement, and developed in good times and bad. The socialist leader Abe Isoo, graduate of the Yale University Divinity School, coached the Waseda University baseball team when his radical politics came under a state ban in the early twentieth century.

It was once believed that the Japanese physique was unsuited to baseball and that Japanese players and Japanese teams would remain forever second-rate. But the Japanese have exploded the myth that they do not have the upper body strength to make the long throw in from the outfield or to pitch the fastball, and they have broken into the lineups of the foremost professional teams in the United States. Irabu Hideki of the New York Yankees throws a fastball that has been clocked at a hundred miles per hour, and in the future we shall surely see more products of the Japanese leagues in American big league stadiums.

Limitations have been placed on American players in Japan, but a few have excelled, most notably Joe Stanka, who pitched three shutouts in the 1964 Japan Series to propel the Nankai Hawks to victory, and Randy Bass, who won the triple batting crown while playing for the Hanshin Tigers in 1984. Both hailed from Oklahoma, Stanka from Waynoka, where the hometown stadium has been named in his honor, and Bass from Lawton, where he is presently engaged in ranching.

One of the most celebrated Americans in the Japanese leagues was Dave Johnson, a second baseman who played well enough for the Yomiuri Giants but found the baseball culture of Japan taxing.

He remembered with dismay that during spring training on an island off southern Kyushu all the players were taken out sixteen miles by bus and told to run back, which he apparently did, but not uncomplainingly. He was also shaken by the Japanese manager's belief that if he failed to hit the first time up, he should be removed from the lineup to spend the game on the bench. Nothing in his experience with the Baltimore Orioles or the Atlanta Braves prepared him for this kind of treatment. Johnson was proud that he had batted just ahead of Henry "Hank" Aaron for the Atlanta Braves and in the position ahead of Oh Sadaharu for the Yomiuri Giants and that "Dave Johnson" is the answer to the trivia question "Who batted in the third slot just ahead of the two greatest home-run hitters of all time?"

Among Japanese players the story of Oh Sadaharu is best known in the United States. He became a celebrity in high school when his team excelled as one of the "sweet sixteen" at Koshien Stadium in Osaka in the tournament that annually transfixes the whole Japanese nation. Controversy accompanied him, and he was barred from another tournament because of his Chinese descent, which made him ineligible for citizenship. Still, he starred in the professional leagues with Japan's most famous team, the Yomiuri Giants, and hit more than eight hundred home runs, surpassing Hank Aaron's total of 755.[11]

Oh's legendary batting coach, Arakawa Hiroshi, drew elements from kabuki theater, Zen religion, and kendō to correct the player's swing; and, after three years of rigorous training, a dramatic improvement occurred, leading to the presumption that Japanese methods applied to baseball could revolutionize the game. In fact, Oh, with his unique flamingo stance at the plate, was probably one of a kind. He played with Japan's highest-profile team during its glory years from 1965 to 1974, when it won the Japan Series every year. When he moved ahead of Aaron's home run total on September 3, 1977, his name began to be recognized in the United States.

Baseball is the national game in both the United States and Japan and provides the best example of the cultural link between the two nations. Japanese prime ministers use baseball similes,

---

[11] William W. Kelly, "Learning to Swing: Oh Sadaharu and the Pedagogy and Practice of Japanese Baseball," in *Learning in Likely Places: Varieties of Apprenticeship in Japan*, ed. John Singleton (Cambridge: Cambridge University Press, 1998), 265–85.

and Prime Minister Kishi Nobusuke realized his boyhood dream by throwing out the first pitch at a Yankees–White Sox game. More recently, on his visit to the United States in May 1999, Prime Minister Obuchi Keizo was pictured throwing the first pitch at a baseball game in Chicago.

The Future?

Numerous binational cultural groups have formed in the five postwar decades of military alliance and high-volume international trade. The jazz communities, the art worlds, the literary crowds, the film devotees, and the baseball players and fans—the ones mentioned here—are only a few of them.

If we look into a crystal ball, we might expect such binational relationships to become more intense. Now that American baseball's hierarchy has admitted that some Japanese players are world class, the next step would be to hold a true world series and to incorporate the winner of the Japan Series into it. The manager of the New York Mets said that he should have pitched Nomo Hideo instead of the man who lost on the final day of the 1998 season, thereby keeping the Mets out of the playoffs; and George Steinbrenner's admiration for the fastball pitcher Irabu was well known. As we go into the twenty-first century, the trans-Pacific baseball relationship, which has been wary, might develop into a series, then into interleague competition, with Americans glued to their TV sets for the outcome of the New York Yankees–Yomiuri Giants game in Tokyo.

A common world culture that embraces both Japan and the United States, however, is an unlikely, and undesirable, development, for it is the differences that attract. George Packard has noted that the "glue" that holds our two nations together is "our fascination with each other and our eagerness to learn from each other."[12]

The framework for this mutual fascination will inevitably change in the twenty-first century. The security treaty that has sent so many Americans to Japan will surely disappear when the problem of divided Korea is resolved. For the first time in a century, China, Japan, and the United States, and even Russia, are on

---

[12] George R. Packard, "Japan Certain to Make the Right Choices," *Japan Times*, first internet article in the series "100 Years, 100 Views." Consulted in September 1998 at <http://www.japantimes.co.jp>.

relatively good terms diplomatically speaking, so just as the
Anglo-Japanese Alliance of 1902 was replaced by the Four Power
Agreement in 1921, so the bilateral treaty will merge into a concert
of the powers, itself a tie that will keep the Japan-U.S. partnership
alive.

The high volume of trans-Pacific trade, which is the second
great support of the relationship, will inevitably continue, but it
may be diluted by a greater Japanese dependence on markets in
Southeast Asia and China. The unnatural separation of Japan
from the great masses of people nearby must end, and, if China's
state-controlled market economy works, then that outlet will inevitably be exploited by Japan. But it will not replace the market in
the United States.

The third factor in the continuing adhesion of the two nations
is the empathy they feel toward one another through their similar
political systems. The benign Occupation, 1945–52, created shared
values of equality, democracy, freedom, economic growth, and a
stable world peace, values unlikely to be undermined any time
soon.

Meanwhile, technology brings us ever closer: fiber-optic cable
allow us to "see" into the other's country, and improvement in
transportation has turned a twenty-nine-hour Pan-American plane
ride, hopping from Hawai'i to Wake Island to Tokyo Haneda in
1956 (my first flight across the Pacific) into an eight-hour flight
from Portland to Tokyo Narita in 1998 (and it will undoubtedly be
telescoped into an hour or two in the next century). Going to
Japan will be the equivalent of traveling to an adjoining state now.

Jazz musicians shuttle across the Pacific regularly; one female
jazz singer who lives in California performs regularly in Tokyo.
Jazz is part of the one-way transmission of Western music to
Japan, but the musical flow may reverse. In a Sunday *New York
Times* we read that "Japan's music may be like Britain's around
1960: on the verge of breaking out" and that "America has begun
to open up to Asian-based popular culture, from *Mulan* to video
games."[13] Those things are clearly for the next generation, not
ours.

The world could change for the worse. The right wing might
come forward in Japan to revive National Spiritual Mobilization;
in the United States the xenophobic element that opposes Asian

---

[13] Neil Strauss, "A Burst of Rock, Bright as the Rising Sun," *New York Times*,
Arts and Recreation Section, July 12, 1998, p. 28.

and Hispanic immigrants, particularly in California, might seize power. Either would alienate the two countries; but democracy allows each nation to correct its errors and excesses, and we must assume the optimistic stance.

Japan could be drawn to Asia, turning its back on the United States, but the Greater East Asia Co-prosperity Sphere turned out not to be so prosperous after all and was formed at a terrible cost in lives abroad and deprivation at home in the 1930s and 1940s. Historical memories inside Japan are vivid enough that the nation is not likely to proceed down that path again any time soon. It is, after all, preferable to make money east across the Pacific than to make war westward in Asia.

American jazz, Japanese painting, Japanese literature, Japanese film, and American baseball will continue to cement the relationship between the two great nations across the Pacific in the twenty-first century. We love one another for our cultural differences, and the cultural strand will link us in the century ahead as much as the economic, security, and political ties.

THREE

Comparative Moral Grammars

RONNIE LITTLEJOHN

In this chapter, I offer a defense of understanding ethics by using comparative moral cultures as the text. I describe the approaches of isolationist absolutism, idealistic romanticism, and comparative pluralism. Using the comparative pluralism model I offer some remarks on the Japanese moral culture. Afterward, I argue that one inference we can draw from such a comparative study is that there is an underlying grammar to the human moral life. Among the features of moral grammar I identify are the presence and use of moral concepts, the function of shame and guilt as behavior controls, the development of a repertoire of excusing conditions, the construction of a stable view of moral character and its formation, the interplay of a tension between principles and relationships, the creation of mechanisms to cope with moral change, and the evolution of a system and style of moral pedagogy and transmission of values. I distinguish between my findings and the view that morality is everywhere the same. I also stress that noticing an underlying moral grammar does not imply necessarily that humans will develop a global moral culture. I conclude by making some observations about the transferability of the new findings on the development of language into the study of human moral cultures.

First, allow me to say what I mean by a moral culture. A moral culture consists of the coherent set of organizing behavioral expectations that set the range of conduct and character that is obligated, prohibited, and permitted for a group of human persons. It is defined by the beliefs and practices that develop out of our need to build relationships for the satisfaction of mutual desires and interests (friendship, mating, kinship, commercial exchange). It develops out of our need to respond to misfortunes, injuries, and even death (tolerance, empathy, sympathy, compassion, and consolation). It represents the way we come to cooperate with each other and reciprocate sharing and giving. And, of course, it is one way we have found to control disharmonious and destructive behavior (lying, deception, abuse, rape, murder). Any given national or ethnic culture may contain one moral culture or more than one, yet a single moral culture may also define many specific national or ethnic cultures.

The values that make up a moral culture do more than guide action. They also inform judgment, choice, evaluation, exhortation, excuse, and rationalization and direct character formation. Since one's moral culture consists of concepts, values, and assumptions about life that are widely shared within that tradition, one can travel within the culture from place to place and meet people unlike oneself and still count on being able to know how to live.

The beliefs and practices that define a moral culture have several traits in common. For a belief or practice to be classified as belonging to a moral culture it must be present in more than one generation. Further, it will typically be regarded in practice as indubitable. We do not expect people to make mistakes about it. We do not expect people to doubt it or argue about it. We do not expect to have to defend it. Rather, it is the assumed foundation from which we make judgments. It will be transmitted through a variety of sources and methods: language, education, stories, media. And, if it is a part of the moral culture, the belief or practice will be changed and modified only slowly and with difficulty.

Understanding the Human Moral Life through Comparative Studies

We may imagine the study of other moral cultures on the analogy of looking through a glass pane in a door at night at someone on the outside. On approaching the door when the light is turned on in the inside entry hall, all you see, if you do not turn on the light outside, is your own reflection, even though you know that someone else is outside. This would be like looking at another moral culture and concluding that it looks just like our own. The reason for this is that when we look out, we see only ourselves because the light from our own culture is so bright that it is reflected back at us.

But if we turn down the light inside and turn on the light outside, we will be able to see the person on the porch more clearly.

We might notice, for instance, that the other does not look just like us at all. This is analogous to turning down our own cultural sensibilities so that we can pay attention to the actual other. It is certainly an improvement over misdescribing the other as looking just like us. But even this approach poses a problem. To return to our analogy, we are still looking through the glass pane of the door. This is tantamount to observing another culture distantly, as a "culture under glass." In this event, we do not really know the other culture any more than we know the person standing on the porch in our example.

Real acquaintance requires that we open the door and make contact. This is true also of the study of comparative moral cultures. A fuller understanding of another culture requires living within it, alongside persons for whom it has been their formative worldview. Every effort should be made to put ourselves into contact with the primary voices of a different culture. Only when this is done can we be reasonably sure that we are beginning to grasp the human form of life found elsewhere.

Our rather simple illustration reveals the steps appropriate in a comparative inquiry. First, we need to identify what beliefs and practices most characterize our own culture and turn down our sensibilities about them. Next, we need to describe what we find in another culture, letting it speak on its own terms. Third, we need to correct, revise, and revisit our assumptions and preconceptions about the other culture in light of what it tells us about itself. Fourth, we need to open the door and immerse ourselves in the other culture, living its form of life as much as possible. Fifth, and finally, we need to listen and learn and live with each other, discovering new ways of being human from each other, thereby growing and enriching our individual and shared lives.

The fact of differences in moral cultures is very clear, in spite of those who claim all cultures are at bottom essentially the same. What one is to make of these differences is much less certain. I believe that the approaches that have been made to the differences of moral culture may be grouped into three different models. The first two models I wish to describe belong to what Martha Nussbaum calls "The Descriptive Vices" in her book *Cultivating Humanity: A Classic Defense of Reform in Liberal Education* (Cambridge: Harvard University Press, 1997, pp. 118–30). The third model I want to describe is that employed in this essay and in my own research into global moral cultures.

The first model is the moral isolationist view. Mary Midgley, in *Heart and Mind* (New York: St. Martin's Press, 1981), has described "moral isolationism" as that view under which the respect and tolerance due from one moral community to another forbids us to criticize any other community's practice. This means that moral isolationism is, strictly speaking, what has been known in the West as a type of ethical relativism. But moral isolationism leads ultimately to a form of skepticism because it suspends comparative judgments of moral cultures, disallowing language about preferred moral beliefs and practices and ruling out in the process any serious cross-cultural dialogue. Michael Featherstone says in his *Undoing Culture: Globalization, Postmodernism and Identity* (London: Sage Publications, 1995), that the postmodernists in the West have actually elevated "otherness" into a strategy for relationships that should be sought out, but he cautions against the cultural and individual atomism that may be the result.

Moral isolationism has the dubious honor of having yielded two of the most strange and disparate outcomes imaginable. On the one hand, some people who have accepted this point of view have gone so far as to give up the right to criticize other communities and to provoke needed moral change. They have abandoned any comparison of moral practices that says one is preferable to another. The result has been a sort of paralysis rooted in noninvolvement in the affairs of other cultures or in the intercultural encounters that are the cartography of our present condition. On the other hand, and at the other extreme, some holding to the moral isolationist position have evolved into absolutists. They have thought that moral cultures do vary in numerous ways, but they have clung to the ethnocentric belief that their own culture has the best or truest morality. This view can be thoroughly documented through the history of Western imperialism and colonialism. Absolutism of this sort is isolationist in the sense that no dialogue with the other is sought because one has come to understand his or her own culture as morally superior and thus has no need to learn from other traditions. Eradication or co-option, not dialogue or conversation, is the goal.

Idealistic romanticism is the second method for approaching the study of comparative cultures that I want to mention. This method focuses on the mysterious and different aspects of another culture. Those beliefs and practices that are common and shared between cultures are ignored. Idealistic romanticism often characterized early Western anthropology, and Orientalism is arguably a good example of it. Idealistic romanticism takes notice in the foreign only of those practices that are different, and it glorifies and even exaggerates these.

Consider the plot of Giacomo Puccini's *Madame Butterfly*. Pinkerton's view of Japanese culture as exotic and totally unlike his own is reflective of a sort of idealistic romanticism. This view leads him to believe that a Japanese woman does not need to be treated with the moral regard he shows his Western wife. The Japanese woman is a delicious plaything, to whom loyalty and promise keeping are entirely unnecessary. But this attitude shows Pinkerton's ignorance of the Japanese moral culture in which women do care profoundly about how they are treated and do not conceive of themselves simply as morsels to be consumed by men.

Idealistic romanticism as a model often oversimplifies cultures with sweeping generalizations; it downplays the complexity and change going on within a culture and its internal tensions. A frequent such mistake often found in the interpretation of Japanese culture is its characterization as homogeneous and nonindividualistic. Certainly Japan has found different ways to express individualism and creativity from those found in the West, but to idealize Japanese culture as merely collective or unreservedly conformist is a serious mistake.

A third model for doing comparative studies takes note not only of the differences between moral cultures, but also of the substantial likenesses between them. This model may be called comparative pluralism. Comparative pluralism does not elevate similar beliefs and practices into some absolutist morality. Neither does it identify likenesses with any one extant culture in the way of ethnocentric imperialism and colonialism. But it does describe a significant shared terrain of material and formal moral practice from which cross-cultural judgments can be made of all particular moralities.

The common moral interests uncovered by comparative pluralism do not have their origin in the blindness of having one's own culture turned up so intensely that all other cultures look really "just like us." These likenesses are contingent, historical, and cultural, not absolute, ontological, or religious. They derive from the grit of human life proved out over generations and stabilized into the great moral cultures that define the lives of humans scattered across the global stage. This common terrain arises from the simple fact that humans wherever they are found have many of the same concerns and that all cultures have found many similar patterns for managing them morally.

The crucial difference between isolationism and comparative pluralism lies in the latter's appreciation for shared morality. Comparative pluralism avoids specifically the undesirable outcome of relativism, which is the inability to make cross-cultural judgments and criticisms. It employs shared moral beliefs and practices as a basis for comparison and criticism. Yet comparative pluralism preserves what is valuable in idealistic romanticism by calling attention to differences between traditions and challenging us to try these on and see if we can learn from other cultures a new way of being that will enrich our lives, one that we can come to value as well.

Turning the Light on Japanese Moral Culture

Unfortunately, time and space do not permit an extensive examination of Japanese moral culture using the comparative pluralism model. However, I want to do two things. First, I want to make some general observations about the moral culture of Japan and how its study helps us understand human moral life in general. Second, I want to model how one might uncover distinctive insights about the material and formal contents of morality in Japan that could be appropriated by other cultures and enhance their conception of human life.

So, first, let me make some general observations about the moral culture of Japan and how its study helps us understand human moral life in general. We can begin by reminding ourselves that Japan's moral culture has been shaped by more than one intellectual and philosophical tributary. Each of the streams of Confucianism, Buddhism, and Shinto has made its own unique contribution to Japan's moral culture. If we pay attention not only to the beliefs and practices taught in these traditions, but also to the way in which they have been made to converse with each other to yield a new culture, then we will learn much about how the sources of moral cultures work in other cultures as well. Here we have found something that Japan can teach us about human moral life in general. Morality is the product of diverse sources that must be brought together in a creative symbiosis.

Japan's moral culture is structured around a web of concepts used to guide behavior and define character. These concepts provide the actual material content of morality as the concepts that name conduct are used for praise and blame. When applied to a person, these concepts name the moral virtues and vices. We can find this same structure in other traditions as well, and indeed many of the moral concepts used in Japan and in other cultures are intertranslatable.

Other ways in which a study of Japan's moral culture helps us understand human moral life in general include its use of an internal machinery of conduct such as intention, deliberation, and purpose; its appreciation for the fact that attempts and omissions are often as important as actions in moral evaluation; its grasp of the ways in which guilt and shame interrelate and of how accident, mistake, and ignorance function as ways of diminishing blame and shame; and finally, its strategies for coping with moral change and internal redirection.

I also promised that I would comment on the many distinctive insights about the material and formal contents of morality in Japan that could be appropriated by other cultures and enhance their conception of human life. I will mention only two.

Studies of Japanese virtue concepts reveal that the following are consistently ranked high: filial piety, industry, tolerance, harmony, loyalty, observation of rites, reciprocation of gifts and favors, kindness, knowledge, solidarity, self-cultivation, appreciation of relationships by status and order, steadiness and stability, resistance to corruption, sincerity, thrift, persistence, patience, a sense of cultural superiority, adaptability, prudence, trustworthiness, a sense of shame, courtesy, and wealth. Concept equivalency studies reveal that these virtues are found in other cultures as well, and are often among the highest ranked also.

Yet the Japanese moral culture has distinctive virtues not easily translatable into the moral languages of other cultures. The widely discussed concept of *amae* is an example. One interpretation of this concept is that it valorizes a sort of conduct that would create a person who anticipates the needs of others and meets them before being asked and even without having to be asked to do so. Such people make relationships highly pleasant. Can human encounters exist and even flourish without instantiating this concept? Probably. But its presence and use represents an insight about what makes relationships run toward intimacy and security that other global moral cultures can learn from the Japanese.

We see that a way of being that is valued in one culture may be discovered and transplanted into another one, thereby expanding the latter's repertoire of forms of life. In the United States, failure to practice *amae* is not morally wrong, because no translatable concept exists for it in English. But if Americans came to use such a concept as a way of taking note of the needs of others and responding to those needs without being told to, or even asked to, the moral life of American culture could be enriched and deepened.

I have time to mention only a second distinctive feature of Japanese morality that might contribute to other moral cultures if appropriated by them. One sees in Japan a highly sophisticated interweaving of the social controls of shame and guilt. A recent work that has brought this to our attention in the West most clearly is William LaFleur's *Liquid Life: Abortion and Buddhism in Japan* (Princeton, N.J.: Princeton University Press, 1992). His discussion of the *mizuko kuyo* rituals clearly indicates that both shame and guilt are active in the moral psychology of the parents who have aborted a fetus. When parents going to temples for the rites have a difficult time facing others, feel a sense of unworthiness, and seek to reclaim worthiness by creative acts rather than by self-punishment, they are displaying behaviors associated with a sense of shame. As they at the same time confess, repay, and seek forgiveness, they are acting out of their guilt. A study of these practices has value far beyond their specific application to abortion. They can offer interesting suggestions to other cultures about the psychological implications of morally significant conduct and what social practices might restore moral equilibrium and interpersonal relationships.

The Underlying Grammar to Human Moral Life

What should we make of the results of a comparative study of Japanese moral culture? Well, I do not think we should rush to make sweeping generalizations based merely on a comparison between Japanese and Western moral cultures. Still, based on this and other comparative studies as well, I hold that we have strong reasons to believe that there is an underlying grammar to human moral life. I think that this grammar has both material and formal elements and that these are tied closely to the sorts of tasks that humans need to perform to survive and flourish. Some of the features of what I call "the grammar of the moral form of life" are the presence and use of moral concepts, the construction of a stable view of moral character, the function of shame and guilt as behavior controls, the development of a repertoire of excusing conditions, the interplay of a tension between principles and relationships, the creation of mechanisms to cope with moral change, and the evolution of a system and style of moral pedagogy and transmission of values.

If we ask about the reasons for belief in a universal moral grammar, the only answer that can be offered is a descriptive one. Study of diverse moral cultures reveals this grammar. Over centuries of evolution humans have developed ingrained desires and aversions, propensities to seek safety and avoid risk, drives to cooperate and seek reciprocation, and feelings of attraction and need for intimacy. These get translated into the interests to direct behavior that are the moral systems humans create. All moral cultures are concerned to control lying and deception. They all interpret intentions based on behavior when language is unavailable. They conceive of each as responsible to the others. They distinguish voluntary and involuntary behavior and diminish blame on the grounds of accident, mistake, and ignorance of consequences. They value empathy. They evaluate behaviors by using both moral rules and role relationships, thereby regulating sexual access and exchange of labor, goods, and services. No moral system is exclusively rule or duty based, any more than one is totally determined by the roles one plays in society. Surely those traditions in the Confucian sphere of influence emphasize one's roles more than one's moral rights or duties, but these latter concerns still have their place even in Confucian ethics. Moral cultures value reciprocity and justice. They contain moral concepts that carry blame of cruelty, rape, murder; and they share a host of virtues and vices in common, even if they might prioritize them differently. They use both shame and guilt to forge character and control behavior, never merely the one and not the other. These kinds of things make up human moral grammar. And the best reason for the belief that there is a universal moral grammar is that these material and formal conditions are found in human ethical systems. They are found in Japanese, Chinese, and Islamic moral cultures just as they are found in the West.

Conclusion

I want to distinguish my claims about a universal moral grammar from three possible misunderstandings. First, I want to dissociate myself from a sort of foundationalism according to which my

views might be taken to mean that the moral grammar or structure I have noticed is a feature of reality in some ontological
sense. This would be like the view taken by the early Wittgen-
stein and many of the Vienna positivists that logic reflected the
scaffolding of reality itself, that it was somehow the internal or
skeletal structure of the world. I do not make this sort of claim
for universal moral grammar. Instead, I hold that the patterns in
moral systems that I have tried to identify are contingent, historical, and cultural, not absolute, ontological, or religious. They have
been formed over generations and stabilized by something like
cumulative natural selection. The patterns exist simply because
humans on a global scale have found them necessary and helpful
for survival and fulfillment.

I also want to make clear that I am not claiming that all moral
cultures have the same beliefs and practices. I certainly do not
believe this. Actual beliefs and practices vary in a way similar to
the way in which actual languages differ. Indeed, this is perhaps
the best analogy I can think of. When one thinks of the recent
work on language we see scholarly consensus moving toward the
view that humans, over a long period of evolution, have
developed a propensity to use language by certain transmitted
patterns that may be called grammatical, while nonetheless having
different linguistic morphologies, phonologies, and vocabularies.
This is what I mean also. Moral cultures work according to the
same sorts of patterns, but they do not, for example, prioritize
their judgments about conduct or about virtues and vices in the
same way nor weigh excusing conditions in the same manner.

The third misunderstanding I would like to avoid is that I am
suggesting that all moral cultures should agree in moral belief and
practice. As world peoples interact more frequently and as communication becomes more comprehensive, the question whether a
growing global moral culture will emerge from our commensur-
able values and interests or whether the sheer weight of difference
will unravel this very concept will be a pressing one. I think that
recognizing the underlying moral grammar of cultures gives us
reason to believe that our shared concerns will enable us to talk
about what forms of conduct and character enrich our lives
together. But we should not think that this dialogue will necessarily create a global morality. In my own view, we need not and
should not seek this either. Many different practices could function as realizations of a common moral interest. So, there is no
reason to seek exact conformity in behavior and practice morally.

Of course, many moral values have carried in the past, and will continue to carry in the future, their own momentum and self-authentication because of the way they contribute to human security and fulfillment. But there are also distinctive ways of being human that vary culturally and that are all morally good. On these matters we can perhaps expect a growing appreciation of the many ways to live a human life in the twenty-first century. Japanese moral culture will certainly play a role in teaching us this truth, as it will also be transformed by it.

FOUR

The Roles of Japanese Corporate Wives in the Globalizing Trend: An Anthropological Perspective

SAWA KUROTANI BECKER

As we enter the new millennium with an anticipation of dramatic changes, the discourse of globalization permeates our turn-of-the-century consciousness. However, the actual effects of globalization on our lives too often seem abstract, ambiguous, and hard to recognize. Ethnography, which emphasizes the "experience-near" observation and analysis of a cultural or social phenomenon at hand (Geertz 1973), provides us a way of peering into the phenomenon of globalization through the concrete experiences of those whose lives have become entangled in the globalizing process. The particular ethnographic situation upon which I focus is the experience of Japanese corporate wives in the United States, those who accompany their spouses assigned to U.S. locations by their Japanese corporate employers. In their gender-ascribed domestic roles, Japanese corporate wives abroad become the boundary markers between Japaneseness and foreignness. These roles, in turn, place them in the key position in Japan's globalization.

Although networks of transcultural relationships have existed in the world for some time (Comaroff and Comaroff 1991; Mintz 1985; Wolf 1982), transnational trends in the last few decades exhibit some unique attributes. "Flexible accumulation," or the spatial and temporal spreading of overaccumulated capital, has increased the mobility of people, goods, and information across national boundaries and has furthered uneven access to technology and wealth on a scale never seen before (Harvey 1989). At the same time, advanced technologies make possible and, indeed, promote the encounter with that which is foreign on a mass scale, with images of the "other" often preceding or even replacing actual encounters (Appadurai 1990; Hannerz 1992; Marcus 1993). Boundaries between nation-states are blurred under these transnational conditions, and the patterns of international migration become increasingly complex and multidirectional. It is common among today's transnational migrants to go back and forth between their home countries and host countries, or to hop from one host country to another, all the while maintaining close economic, cultural, and personal ties with their origins (Basch, Schiller, and Blanc 1994).

Foreign travel and migration of Japanese nationals today differ significantly from the mass emigration to North America at the end of the nineteenth century and in the first decades of the twentieth century. While earlier Japanese immigrants, by and large from a rural background and motivated by the promise of economic opportunities, formed a well-defined minority group in the United States (e.g., Kitano 1969), *shin-issei*, or the new Japanese immigrants who arrived in the United States after World War II, include people with diverse backgrounds and a wide range of motives, and their migration behavior is much more fluid (Ishi 1989; Shimasaki 1988). Japanese newcomers also tend to form their own subgroups in the United States and to maintain strong ties with Japan or expatriate corporate Japanese communities, apart from existing *nikkei*, or Japanese-American, communities (Ishi 1989; Ishitoya 1991).

Many contemporary Japanese newcomers to the United States are, however, neither "immigrants," who live in the host country permanently, nor "travelers," who go abroad for a limited duration. These newcomers usually intend to stay in the United States for a certain period of time and then return to Japan. Young Japanese who quit their schools and jobs in Japan and come to the United States for language studies or career upgrading would fall into this category (Ishitoya 1991; Kawa 1991). So do expatriate Japanese workers and their families who are sent to the United States on job assignments.

Kaigai chuuzai, an assignment—or the state of being assigned— at a remote post overseas, has been an important personnel practice for Japanese corporations with overseas business interests (Hamada 1992). *Kaigai chuuzai* in the United States became particularly important with Japan's postwar economic recovery, as Japanese corporations found consumers of their products in the affluent U.S. market. As challenging as it might have been, *Amerika chuuzai* (a job assignment in the United States) throughout the 1950s and 1960s had its rewards. It was a rare and prestigious opportunity that signaled the fast-track career and promised a higher standard of living both during and after the assignment.

Through the 1970s and 1980s, the patterns of *Amerika chuuzai* changed dramatically. With the rapid expansion of Japanese business interests and direct investment in the United States through these decades, the number of *kaigai chuuzaiin*, or expatriate Japanese corporate employees, steadily increased; in fact, it is estimated to have more than doubled through the 1980s (Japanese Ministry of Foreign Affairs 1997). At the same time, the types of *chuuzaiin* diversified, from mostly white-collar, elite-track employees of major corporations in trading, finance, and sales, to more technically oriented workers of medium and small-sized corporations in the manufacturing sector (MITI 1996). The locations to which these expatriate workers are assigned also spread from large metropolitan areas along the two coasts to midsized cities and smaller towns in the Midwest and Southeast, where there were historically very few Asian minorities (e.g., Hettinger and Tooley 1994; Kim 1995).

With the expansion of Japanese corporate activities in the United States, the significance of *kaigai chuuzai* has also begun to erode: it is no longer a prestigious sign of "elite status" or "fast-track career," but increasingly a commonplace, and often mandatory, aspect of a Japanese corporate worker's lifelong career. At the same time, tangible benefits of *kaigai chuuzai* have decreased, as the economic disparity between Japan and the United States shrank rapidly and Japanese corporations began to cut back on financial support for their *kaigai chuuzaiin*. In many situations I encountered during my ethnographic fieldwork, *kaigai chuuzai* was considered to have little significance in one's career advancement; in some others, it was outright harmful because long years abroad might make an expatriate worker "out of touch" with changing business situations in Japan (also see Hamada 1992; Kim 1995).

As an increasing number of Japanese corporate workers go abroad on the job, their wives are also asked—directly by the corporations or indirectly through their husbands—to accompany their *chuuzaiin* husbands and create "Japanese" homes for them in a foreign environment. I became interested in the experience of Japanese corporate wives abroad because of the unique position that they occupy as homemakers at the intersection of Japan's "global" versus "local" or economic versus cultural interests. While their feminine roles, as wives and mothers, make them responsible for cultural reproduction at home, their homemaking labor is exported outside Japan to serve the interests of Japanese transnational corporations whose success is increasingly dependent on their overseas operations.

Both academic and popular Japanese discourses have tended to define *uchi* (an inside, a home, or "the self") as a stable location of Japanese identity. Thus, in much of the academic literature, Japanese "relational" selves are seen as nurtured within this "in-group," where its members share a sense of familiarity, comfort, and belonging (Bachnik and Quinn 1994; Doi 1973; Nakane 1967; Smith 1983). Some of the recent studies on Japanese identities question such a static notion of *uchi*, however, and reconceptualize it as an unstable domain in which desirable Japanese subjectivity is constructed in contrast to the opposing domain of *soto* (an outside, a strange place, or the "other") (Allison 1994; Kondo 1990). Japanese companies often appropriate this concept of *uchi* to promote corporate solidarity and to ensure the loyalty and productivity of their workers (Rohlen 1974).

Normative division of labor dictates that *uchi*/home is women's domain, and the domestic management and child care the sole responsibility of wives and mothers (Imamura 1987; Iwao 1993). Although naturalized in the Japanese ideology of gender differences, this association between Japanese women and domesticity is a relatively recent historic phenomenon. The rapid development of heavy industry in Japan in the early 1900s relied upon the recruitment of men as industrial workers, leaving women to manage the household. Thus, homes of the emerging wage-earning middle class became increasingly "feminized" and were incorporated into the economic machinery of a fast-growing capitalist nation (Hara 1989; Koyama 1994; Ueno 1987).

In today's era of increasing globalization, Japanese women's domestic labor is the key to managing the paradox of *kaigai chuuzai*. Japanese multinational corporations need workers who are international enough to function well in a foreign environment, but not so cosmopolitan that they lose their steadfast loyalty to their companies and their country (cf. White 1992; Yanagihara 1994). Outside the physical boundary of the nation and away from well-established institutions of corporate socialization (Allison 1994; Yoshino 1992), domestic space becomes a primary location of identity maintenance for corporate workers and their children, a space where the complex relationship with the foreign other is managed and the integrity of their "Japaneseness" is protected. Japanese corporate wives are, thus, positioned to safe-guard the identity of their family members against a foreign other, as an extension of their ascribed feminine roles as homemakers.

Between the global ambition of Japanese capitalism and the cultural ideology of Japaneseness, the expatriate Japanese wives whom I encountered during my fieldwork in three U.S. cities took their responsibilities as wives and mothers seriously and labored hard to help their families cope with transnational migration. Their "maintenance" work ranged from the creation of familiar "Japanese" domestic space, where their husbands and children could relax after a day in foreign workplaces and schools, to being there, both physically and psychologically, to provide support for their families under extreme stress. The sense of duty and obliga-tion permeated the discourse of *kaigai chuuzai* among my corporate-wife informants, who seemed to unfailingly put the wel-fare of their husbands and children before their own. They rarely questioned or contested the gendered assignment of domestic responsibilities, as they assumed that housework and child care came with the territory, so to speak, and often defined their femi-ninity through their domesticity and motherliness. Thus, their self-construct and gender-role expectations appeared at first to conform to the assertion in the existing literature that other-orientation and the fulfillment of gender roles are the central com-ponents of Japanese women's selfhood (e.g., Iwao 1993; Lebra 1984).

However, transnational migration seemed to have had unex-pected effects on Japanese corporate wives' understanding of their gender roles and identities. My inquiries revealed that my infor-mants did not necessarily expect their domesticity to be a reliable source of self-definition and that they resisted the imposition of domesticity as the sole purpose of their lives abroad. In Japan, they often sought the senses of accomplishment and self-identity through activities not directly related to domestic chores—for instance, friendship with other women, volunteer activities, and part-time jobs—that took them outside the domestic space and got them in touch with the larger social world (also Lebra 1984; Yoshi-take 1994). A foreign assignment for most Japanese wives meant disruption or difficulty in the process of self-fulfillment outside the home. Their visa status as dependents made paid jobs out of the question, and their lack of communication skills precluded most volunteer possibilities, too. Children's futures became more pre-carious than ever during the prolonged foreign residence, and many mothers found themselves ill-equipped to help their children. Many expatriate Japanese wives work hard to network with other Japanese wives, yet the transiency of *chuuzai* life makes these networks fragile and hard to maintain. The *ningen kankei*, or human relationships, are often complicated and cumbersome in closed expatriate communities, and may stifle their social life overseas (also Mori and Saike 1997).

As the avenues of social participation suddenly dropped out of these women's lives, and domesticity became inflated as the essence of their feminine selves during their *kaigai chuuzai*, many expatriate wives found their senses of self flattened, lopsided, and incomplete. A number of my female informants seemed conscious of the negative effect of imposed domesticity and expressed dissatisfaction with their lives overseas that tended to confine them in their *uchi*. In these moments of doubt, some began to question the very gender roles that they took for granted in Japan.

In the meantime, the relationship between the women's domestic labor and their husbands' world of work becomes clearer than ever in the expatriate household and appears to blur the distinctions between *uchi* and *soto*. To fulfill their "domestic" roles, expatriate Japanese wives have to venture out to the foreign *soto*, acquire a substantial amount of local knowledge, and network with other Japanese wives, and sometimes with local Americans, for information, support, and advice, much more so than do their husbands, who spend most of their time abroad within a Japan-based corporate structure. The organization of expatriate work life also requires the husbands to bring work-related activities into their homes (also Fukunaga 1990; Taniguchi 1985). So, again, in their "domestic" roles, wives receive after-hours business calls, entertain business guests, and come to know their husband's world of work better than they did in Japan, where the physical and psychological separation of work and home is more complete (Beck and Beck 1994). In addition, many corporations explicitly tell their expatriate wives that it is these women's duty overseas to manage and maintain their husband's productivity and to serve as hostesses for corporate clients and visitors. These tasks are, in turn, stated as the sole justification for the spousal benefits during *kaigai chuuzai*, thus betraying the relationship between the corporate economic agenda and women's homemaking labor (see Fukunaga 1990; Okifuji 1986).

The *chuuzai* in the United States also meant a break from social restrictions placed on middle-class families back in Japan. Away from the intervention of the extended family and the corporate socialization practices that kept married couples apart for most of their waking hours, expatriate husbands and wives spent more time together at home and often found support and companionship in each other for the first time in their marriage. The wife's increased involvement with the husband's work life, and the husband's increased involvement at home, could create a sense of more egalitarian partnership between them as well. A surprising number of informants also commented that the parent-child relationships improved through *kaigai chuuzai* as they faced the difficult transition together as a family (cf. Saito 1987).

At the same time, the exposure to an American way of life gives expatriate wives alternative views on aspects of their lives that they accepted as natural and inevitable: the relationship with their husbands and children, the notion of "home," and the meaning of being "Japanese." After many years of foreign residence, many corporate Japanese families begin to wonder where their *uchi*/home really is. Even when they intend to return to Japan after their *chuuzai* assignments, they grow attached to their foreign "homes" even to the extent that their homecoming to Japan becomes quite difficult (see also White 1992). Many of my informants also noted high quality of life, partnership between the husband and wife, and the value of private life over work life, for example, as positive attributes of middle-class American life and wondered whether their Japanese way of life could be changed. Some of my informants actually used the examples of their American neighbors to initiate such a change.

The changing notions of home and self are also evident in the actions of some women who began to explore their own paths during the *kaigai chuuzai*. Some wives chose to live in the United States permanently, with or without their husbands. Some women rekindled their intellectual interests and went back to school. A couple of women started international businesses, which grew out of their activities as expatriate wives. These women began to redefine themselves through transnational migration; they became the agents of their own lives, rather than spouses of international businessmen and reluctant transmigrants who had no goals of their own.

It appears that Japanese corporations and academic observers have made similar mistakes when they assumed the stability of *uchi* and the singular importance of domesticity in Japanese women's lives. The examples of Japanese wives who modified their notions of *uchi* and feminine selves indicate that the exposure to foreign cultures may have transformative effects even on those who are slated conservative roles in a society where diversion from the norm is often unacceptable. This, then, is the biggest irony of *kaigai chuuzai:* by delegating the identity-maintenance tasks to the domestic sphere and exposing *uchi* to a foreign *soto*, transnational corporations may have inadvertently transformed their corporate subjects' sense of *uchi*, thus undermining their own structure of power from inside out (Bourdieu 1977).

Japan has had ambivalent relationships with the world, and more specifically with its Western others for some 140 years, since it was rudely awakened from its feudal isolation in 1854 (Hosoya and Homma 1991; Miyoshi and Harootunian 1993). Although its push for internationalization has produced some tangible results in the areas of national policies and corporate organizations, the further stages of internationalization, namely the transformation of cultural values and individual actions (Mannari and Befu 1983), are yet to happen. If Japan is to become one day a nation of people with truly "global" consciousness, expatriate Japanese wives and mothers may have a significant role to play in that process. As homemakers, they can bring home their transnational experience and introduce new ideas and identities into the location of Japanese cultural identity, the individual homes of ordinary Japanese citizens. Thus far, the reality that *kaigai chuuzai* returnees and their families face back home has been neither easy nor comfortable. The mark of "foreignness" is too often met with indifference at best, alarm and even rejection in the worst cases (Osawa 1986; White 1992). Many wives and mothers who participated in my research knew this harsh reality and voiced concerns about what would happen to their children, their husbands, and themselves upon their return to Japan. If they are able to hold on to the liberating insights from their transnational migration and resist the pressure to conform, to fall back onto the conservative path laid out for themselves and their families, then they are making an invaluable contribution to Japan's, and the world's, twenty-first century.

References Cited

Allison, Anne. 1994. *Nightwork: Sexuality, Pleasure and Corporate Masculinity in a Tokyo Hostess Club.* Chicago: University of Chicago Press.

Appadurai, Arjun. 1990. "Disjuncture and Difference in the Global Cultural Economy." *Public Culture* 2(2):1–24.

———. 1991. "Global Ethnoscapes: Notes and Queries." In *Recapturing Anthropology,* ed. Richard Fox. Santa Fe, N.M.: School of American Research Press.

Bachnik, Jane, and Charles Quinn, Jr., eds. 1994. *Situated Meanings: Inside and Outside in Japanese Self, Society, and Language.* Princeton, N.J.: Princeton University Press.

Basch, Linda; Nina Glick Schiller; and Cristina Szanton Blanc. 1994. *Nations Unbound: Transnational Projects, Postcolonial Predicaments, and Deterritorialized Nation-States.* Langhorn, Penn.: Gordon and Breach.

Beck, John, and Martha Beck. 1994. *The Change of a Lifetime: Employment Patterns among Japan's Managerial Elite.* Honolulu: University of Hawai'i Press.

Bourdieu, Pierre. 1977. *Outline of a Theory of Practice.* Cambridge: Cambridge University Press.

Comaroff, Jean, and John Comaroff. 1991. *Of Revelation and Revolution: Christianity, Colonialism, and Consciousness in South Africa.* Vol. 1. Chicago: University of Chicago Press.

Doi, Takeo. 1973. *Anatomy of Dependence.* Trans. John Bester. Tokyo: Kodansha International.

Fukunaga Tatsuko. 1990. *Aruhi Kaigai Funin* (One day, a foreign transfer). Tokyo: Japan Times.

Geertz, Clifford. 1973. *The Interpretation of Cultures.* New York: Basic Books.

Gupta, Akhil, and James Ferguson. 1992. "Beyond 'Culture': Space, Identity, and the Politics of Difference." *Cultural Anthropology* 7(1):6–23.

Hamada, Tomoko. 1992. "Under the Silk Banner: The Japanese Company and Its Overseas Managers." In *Japanese Social Organization,* ed. Takie Sugiyama Lebra. Honolulu: University of Hawai'i Press.

Hannerz, Ulf. 1992. "The Global Ecumene as a Network of Networks." In *Conceptualizing Society,* ed. Adam Kuper. New York: Routledge.

Hara Hiroko. 1989. *Katei no Keiei* (Home management). Tokyo: Nihon Hoso Shuppan Kyokai.

Harvey, David. 1989. *The Condition of Postmodernity.* Cambridge, Mass.: Blackwell.

Hettinger, James, and Stanley Tooley. 1994. *Small Town, Giant Corporation: Japanese Manufacturing Investment and Community Economic Development in the United States.* Lanham, Md.: University Press of America.

Hosoya Chihiro and Homma Yagayo, eds. 1991. *Nichibei Kankeishi Shinban: Masatsu to Kyocho no 140nen* (History of U.S.-Japan relations, new edition: 140 years of conflict and cooperation). Tokyo: Yuikaku.

Imamura, Anne. 1987. *Urban Japanese Housewives.* Honolulu: University of Hawai'i Press.

Ishi Tomotsugu. 1989. "Shin-issei towa Nanika" (What is new *issei?*). *Nobiru-Kai 15th Anniversary Issue,* September, 35–40.

Ishitoya Shigeru. 1991. *Nihon wo Suteta Nihonjin* (The Japanese who abandoned Japan). Tokyo: Soushisha.

Iwao, Sumiko. 1993. *The Japanese Woman: Traditional Image and Changing Reality.* New York: Free Press.

Japanese Ministry of Foreign Affairs. 1997. *Kaigai Zairyuu Houjin Ninzuu Chousa Toukei* (Statistics on the number of expatriate Japanese). Tokyo: Japanese Ministry of Foreign Affairs.

Kawa Emi. 1991. *Kanojo ga Nyuu Yoku ni Itta Wake* (The reason why she went to New York City). Tokyo: PHP Kenkyujo.

Kim, Choong Soon. 1995. *Japanese Industry in the American South.* New York: Routledge.

Kitano, Harry. 1969. *Japanese Americans: The Evolution of a Subculture.* Englewood Cliffs, N.J.: Prentice Hall.

Kondo, Dorinne. 1990. *Crafting Selves.* Chicago: University of Chicago Press.

Koyama, Shizuko. 1994. "The 'Good Wife and Wise Mother' Ideology in Post–World War I Japan." *U.S.-Japan Women's Journal: English Supplement* 7:31–52.

Lebra, Takie Sugiyama. 1984. *Japanese Women.* Honolulu: University of Hawai'i Press.

Mannari, Hiroshi, and Harumi Befu, eds. 1983. *The Challenge of Japan's Internationalization: Organization and Culture.* Seminar Proceedings, Kwansei Gakuin University, Sengari Seminar House, June 30–July 5, 1981. Nishinomiya, Hyoko, Japan: Kwansei Gakuin University.

Marcus, George, ed. 1993. *Perilous States: Conversations on Culture, Politics and Nation.* Chicago: University of Chicago Press.

MITI (Japanese Ministry of International Trade and Industry). 1996. *Summary of "The Survey of Trends in Overseas Business Activities of Japanese Companies."* Tokyo: International Business Affairs Division, Ministry of International Trade and Industry.

Mintz, Sydney. 1985. *Sweetness and Power: The Place of Sugar in Modern History.* New York: Viking.

Miyoshi, Masao, and H. D. Harootunian, eds. 1993. *Japan in the World.* Durham, N.C.: Duke University Press.

Mori Rie and Hibari Saike. 1997. *Chuuzaiin Fujin no Deepu na Sekai* (The deep world of expatriate wives). Tokyo: Media Factory.

Nakane Chie. 1967. *Tate Shakai no Ningen Kankei: Tanitsu Shakai no Riron* (Human relations in vertical society: A theory of singular society). Tokyo: Kodansha.

Osawa Chikako. 1986. *Tattahitotsu no Aoi Sora* (The one and only blue sky). Tokyo: Bungeishunju.

Okifuji Noriko. 1986. *Tenkinzoku no Tsumatachi* (The wives of the corporate transfer tribe). Osaka: Sougensha.

Saito Shigeta. 1987. *Chichioya Fuzai Sindoromu* (Paternal absence syndrome). Tokyo: Yomiuri Shimbunsha.

Shimasaki, Kana. 1988. "The Characteristics and Problems of Japanese Newcomers." *Yellow Journal* 2(2):7–11.

Smith, Robert. 1983. *Japanese Society.* Cambridge: Cambridge University Press.

Rohlen, Thomas. 1974. *For Harmony and Strength: Japanese White-Collar Organization in Anthropological Perspective.* Berkeley: University of California Press.

Taniguchi, Etsuko. 1985. *Madam Shosha.* Tokyo: Gakuseisha.

Ueno, Chizuko. 1987. "Genesis of the Urban Housewife." *Japan Quarterly*, April–June, 130–42.

White, Merry. 1992. *The Japanese Overseas: Can They Go Home Again?* Princeton, N.J.: Princeton University Press.

Wolf, Eric. 1982. *Europe and the People without History.* Berkeley: University of California Press.

Yanagihara Kazuko. 1994. *"Zaigai" Nihonjin* ("Expatriate" Japanese). Tokyo: Shobunsha.

Yoshino, Kosaku. 1992. *Cultural Nationalism in Contemporary Japan: A Sociological Inquiry.* New York: Routledge.

Yoshitake Teruko, ed. 1994. *Nihon no Kazoku wo Kangaeru* (Thinking about the Japanese family). Kyoto: Mineruva Shobou.

FIVE

Health Care in Twenty-first-Century Japan

VICTORIA DOUGLASS

What will health care in Japan be like in the twenty-first century? What kinds of transformations will occur in health care? What will be the main sources of transformation? What will influence the changes? The answers to these questions can help to forecast the development of a service crucial to any nation. Asking and attempting to answer the questions can allow us to better focus on the present and the future of the nation. A few major elements will shape the transformation of health care services and facilities. Primary among these elements are the aging of the population, the growing use of technology, economic considerations, and the results of research into the relationship between the environment of care and patient outcomes.

Health care developed differently in Japan and in the United States. Traditional Chinese medicine was imported into Japan and practiced in the court beginning in the sixth century. A German model of health care education and provision was adopted in 1870 (Hashimoto 1973). In the United States during colonial times care was given in the home. Later a model for providing health care primarily influenced by the model of care developed in Western Europe and by the military model was accepted (Thompson 1975). In Japan, some elements from the United States were incorporated into the Japanese health care system after 1945. Advances in health care in the last century have had far-reaching effects. The development of the germ theory of disease, antiseptics, sterilization, inoculation, analgesics, x-rays, and the abandonment of such measures as bleeding, overdosing, and purging transformed medicine (Thompson 1975). These elements transformed health care much as ultrasonics, CAT and PET scans, noninvasive and micro surgery, and telemedicine continue to transform it today and much as gene therapy, cloning, cultivation of material for transplantation, and more refined imaging methods will transform it tomorrow.

Recent study shows measurable relationships between the environment of care and patient outcomes (Rubin, Owens, and Golden 1998). The outcomes affected included physical, anatomical, and physiological health; diagnoses; adverse events; and complications. The environment of care also affects patient evaluation of health and of health care. Health facilities traditionally emphasized functional efficiency rather than supportive settings for patient care (Ulrich 1984). This emphasis has produced sterile, psychologically "hard" facilities that tend to increase stress for both patients and staff. People in health care facilities more than in many other types of buildings need opportunities for visual release to reduce stressful situations. Stress resulting from poor design has been implicated in increased anxiety, depression, high blood pressure, and social withdrawal (Ulrich 1991). Possibly, as designers recognize the importance of this research they will produce more patient-friendly and humane designs.

Many elements of the environment outside of design affect the provision of health care. Some of those include the growing proportion of elders and the increasing use of computer technology. One of the most vital demographic forces effecting Japan today is the aging of its population. People live longer in Japan than in any other country. By 2025 more than one in four people in Japan will be sixty-five years or older (Gunji 1996). This is a revolutionary event. Never in peacetime has there been such a great number of elders in a population. Along with aging, the population in Japan is highly educated, and more people are comfortable with a higher level of technology than in many countries. Because there is a technology-friendly population, use of high technology to extend scarce human resources in the health care field will be more readily accepted in Japan than elsewhere.

In 1998 a smaller proportion of elders lived with their families than before, and the number of elders living other than within the family is likely to increase. This trend was not apparent as little as twenty years ago (Linhart 1984). Pressures that add to this trend include a return of women to the workforce and meager living space in urban areas. Women must work after marriage in greater numbers than formerly, and so more frequently there is no ready companionship for an aged parent in the home. When an elder goes to the hospital for an illness, often the small living space within the home is redistributed so there is no place to which this person may return upon leaving the hospital. The elder is housed in a retirement home or perhaps finds lodging elsewhere. This choice—to remove elders from the family home—is certain to reduce the richness of the experience of family life. Also the community's opinion of a family who has a parent in the hospital is different from the opinion of a family who has a parent in an alternative care situation.

Housing elders outside the family home also affects health care facilities. Hospitals keep elderly patients after they have recuperated because they have no home to which to return. The low cost of a hospital bed is not so much that it is a burden for most families. This service to the families of old people increases the average length of a hospital stay. In Japan the the average length of a hospital stay is 33.5 days (Ministry of Health 1998) compared to 6.3 days (USDHHS 1997) in the United States. In the United States nonacute care for the elderly is more often separated into nursing home, skilled nursing, or long-term care units, and those functions and statistics are kept separate from acute care. In Japan care of the recuperated elderly is not separated from the rest of the acute care hospital either statistically or physically. While this situation prevents accurate comparison, it allows for easy management of existing bed space and staff. When the hospital census is low, staff do not hurry to discharge patients who are less acutely ill. When the hospital is full, elderly patients or the less acutely ill can be discharged more quickly by resident physicians. Nevertheless, pressure to reduce the relatively high average length of a hospital stay in Japan will increase because of concern for economic performance. Reducing costs for care will remain an issue well into the twenty-first century.

In the twenty-first century, where there is sufficient room for elders in the home, care may be needed for them over a longer period. Research shows that elders in the United States prefer to remain in their homes and that it is better for them to do so, when possible. Perhaps there will be more home health care services provided to elders in the future in Japan. The number of patients discharged to home health care has been rising in the United States (Dey 1995). Discharge to home health care has been effective in reducing nursing home use by the elderly and reducing the strain on employed caregivers (Seidl 1983). The use of high-cost care associated with home care has been relatively rare in the United States. The provision of home health care services reduces the burden on family and other caregivers and improves their relationship with the elderly (MaloneBeach 1992).

In the United States the greatest number of health care services are used by those in the last thirty days of life. It is likely that this pattern is similar in Japan. This means that the health care facility of the future must not only be accessible to seniors in the fullest meaning of the term, it must be designed to meet their needs. It needs greater sensitivity to wayfinding, physical accessibility, and lighting design with particular emphasis on avoiding glare and on older eyes' ability to perceive color. It also means that the building and its furnishings must be designed to enable elders to use the facility fully. Unfortunately, much of the other infrastructure in Japan is not accessible. It is very rare to see people in wheelchairs in the subway or commuter trains in the cities. Many of the stations have no access for other than able-bodied riders. Many buildings similarly have no handicapped access. This is less of a problem for an elder accompanied by a young relative; but as elders are removed from the family home, the escort will become less frequent. More unaccompanied elders will require more infrastructure support both in and out of the health care facility to continue to be mobile and active.

Computer diagnosing and automated provision of services is a development of health care services to extend scarce human resources. Japan's well-educated, high-technology-friendly population makes it possible for this technique to extend care to the underserved. Science fiction shows physicians who wave a small hand-held apparatus over the patient and the illness or wound is healed. Looking at the advances in current telemedicine technology, one sees that for certain procedures the physician need not be in the same location as the patient. Currently in the United States diagnostic imaging, analysis of a patient's vital signs, communication, and consultation can take place with the patient and attending physician at a rural hospital and the expert diagnostician in an urban medical institution. This freedom of access to consultation with specialists allows people from medically underserved areas access to the same quality of care available to those who live in large metropolitan centers. It allows physicians more accurate, comprehensive consultation with specialists on difficult or unfamiliar cases. Japan has emerging centers of telemedicine practice, but the emphasis has so far been to export services to less-developed parts of Asia rather than to intensify use of the techniques within the country. If one were to pair this technology with existing computer-driven medical diagnostic programs, it is possible to imagine the ambulatory care center of the future as much like an automated-teller kiosk. The patient could insert a coded record card, the vital signs would be detected and charted, the patient would answer a series of pertinent questions, and a prescription would be issued for medication, therapy, or other services or an appointment could be made for a personal interview with a practitioner. Or perhaps these services would be available on demand in the home as telephone and Internet services are now. Some kinds of services may be replaced by less traumatic means of treatment, such as breast cancer surgery being replaced by gene therapy, or prostate surgery replaced by microwave therapy, or major surgery replaced by laparoscopy or microsurgery. Scenarios such as these reduce the use of the hospital and help to separate the provision of health care services from the high-cost facilities that house them today.

Still, high-cost facilities are likely to be evident in the twenty-first century. One type that may emerge in Japan is the "Freisen concept" hospital. This kind of hospital was introduced to the United States in the middle of the twentieth century and has been less successful than it could be. The aim of the concept was to reduce the constant need for labor in hospitals by adding mechanical systems that carried out the menial repetitive tasks not connected to direct patient care. Linens, meals, drugs, and supplies were sorted, packaged, and transported to each unit; and reusable items, waste, and soiled linen were removed by automated systems. Relieved of such duties, the hospital staff could spend time on patient care rather than on stocking and transport. It is possible that these early hospitals met with only limited success because of the demands for reliability in operation of the systems and because of the embryonic state of the art of the systems at the time of introduction. Hospital systems require reliability. To delay administration of a drug, a dressing, or a procedure because a mechanical system is malfunctioning compromises care. Early installations were maintenance-intensive, and few hospitals had the necessary trained maintenance personnel available to ensure continuous smooth operation. In 1998 a new hospital was built in Kawasaki, Japan, using Freisen concept techniques for transportation and logistics. Perhaps the advanced state of the art, training of maintenance personnel by producers of these systems, and training of hospital staff in the use of the systems will allow this facility to realize success not seen elsewhere. If this hospital proves successful, the implications for the hospital of the future could be far-reaching. As mechanical systems become more sophisticated through successive improvements in technology, it is possible that their use could extend into direct patient care. Robotic care for infectious patients or for delicate surgical techniques could be developed from existing techniques. People in the twentieth century who are ill still have a need for contact with other human beings for comfort and reassurance, but perhaps that need will change as we grow further and further estranged from the natural world and more dependent on computer technology.

Japanese hospitals have low acuity levels and low staff-to-patient ratios compared to U.S. hospitals. An easy comparison to make is in childbirth since the function is similar in both countries. In Japan women are commonly scheduled to stay in the hospital for seven days for childbirth; in the United States, by contrast, many women who are patients of health maintenance organizations (HMOs) are allowed twenty-four to forty-eight hours for an uncomplicated delivery. Given that the calculation of average length of stay includes women in childbirth, it is likely that the patients in Japanese hospitals are less acutely ill. This disparity in average length of stay may change as a result of economic pressures. Despite the renowned Japanese orientation to providing excellent service, perhaps people will be asked to continue their recuperation at home when the acute phase of the illness is past. As the average length of a hospital stay is reduced and people depend less on the hospital as the location for all of their health care needs, more bed space will become vacant and will remain vacant longer. Such vacancy rates will allow some of the five thousand plus hospitals in Japan to close as the facilities age and become less efficient. Staff-to-patient ratios in Japanese hospitals are one to one, while in U.S. hospitals there are three or more staff to one patient. Low staff-to-patient ratios will probably increase as patient acuity and the resulting demands on the staff for care increase.

Medicine as a caring profession rather than as a money-making enterprise is still the dominant model in Japan as it was before 1945 in the United States. Health care in the two countries differs in other ways, too. In Japan universal coverage of health insurance for all citizens was achieved in 1961. A few large organizations, including the government, provide payment for health care. In the United States there are many insurers. These organizations negotiate with providers to reduce costs or to

influence the care extended to their subscribers to lower the cost
of providing care, but this negotiation does not improve care,
which is not accessible to all or even to all employed Americans
and their families. At least 39 million Americans have no coverage for medical expenses, while one in four is regularly uninsured
for some time (Afifi 1996)—and the rate is growing. In the United
States, health care was 13.6 percent of the gross domestic product
for 1995 while in Japan 6.9 percent of the gross national product
was spent on health care (USDHHS 1997). Clearly, health care in
Japan is a better value.

It may be that the difference in the orientation of Japanese
toward health care as a right of the people, rather than as a service for those who can afford it, has its roots in the differences
between the Japanese population and the U.S. population. In
Japan the population is mostly Japanese. There has been a long
history of low migration into Japan. A long history of isolation
has made Japan's originally ethnically diverse (Hashimoto 1973)
population somewhat more uniform. The United States, in contrast, has a population of diverse ethnic heritage—one of the most
diverse in the world. Perhaps the basis for the profit motive lies
in the difference between the relatively cohesive Japanese population and the extremely diverse U.S. population. It may be acceptable to profit from the misery of other groups in a diverse population while it may be perceived as less than ethical to profit from
the misery of "our own" people in a more closely knit society. In
a parallel development within the U.S. health care facility, occa-
sionally one department may have so many patients and consume
so many of the hospital's resources that it expands until there is
little competition to its own mission. When this occurs, much of
the rest of the facility exists to serve that department. How does
this element of health care organizational development transform
into the twenty-first century? In the United States, health care
facilities have been specialized to meet the needs of individual
segments of the population. This specialization has allowed
development of centers-of-excellence that focus on one area of
practice. Cancer centers, burn centers, women's centers, surgery
centers, and birthing centers are a few of the kinds of facilities that
have resulted from this kind of medical specialization. The result
in the quality of care provided by the improvements these centers
have provided ensures that specialization of health care facilities
will spread. Perhaps the creation of centers-of-excellence could

allow Japan to build a reputation for specialized care that it can then market to the rest of Asia and the world.

Forces that will affect the transformation of health care of the future in Japan included the aging population, technical advances in health care and in materials handling, advances in computer and communications technology, the orientation of Japanese toward health care as a caring profession, and the opportunity to develop specialized health care centers. To a great extent the aging of Japan's population will drive the transformation of its health care facilities. They will have to be made more accessible to elders as will much of the new and existing infrastructure. Health care facilities in the future will be far more technologically active, while the technology will become more imbedded within the structure and subordinated to the need to provide patients and staff with a supportive environment in which to work and to heal. More health care will be provided at home. Telemedicine's "teledoc units" or dial-up physician or diagnostician contact may allow the majority of ambulatory care to be provided at home. Automated hospitals will reduce the need for staff to perform other than direct patient care tasks. Some tasks of direct patient care may be performed by robotic devices. Health care within Japan will remain a caring profession that serves the citizens rather than becoming an economic profit center. The development of centers-of-excellence recognized for outstanding care in specialty areas may become an export commodity and a driver of economic growth. Many other scenarios for the future may be developed from these elements of the existing situation. The whole is greater than the sum of the parts, and it is likely that actual development will be affected by discoveries that are yet in the future.

Bibliography

Afifi, A.; Breslow, L.; and Brown, E. 1996. "United States." In *International Handbook of Public Health*, ed. K. Hurrelmann and U. Laaser. London: Greenwood Press.

Dey, A. 1995. "Characteristics of Elderly Men and Women Discharged from Home Health Care Services: United States, 1991–92." In *Advance Data from Vital and Health Statistics*, no. 259. Hyattsville, Md.: U.S. Department of Health and Human Services, National Center for Health Statistics.

Hashimoto, M. 1973. "Japan." In *Health Services Prospects: An International Survey*, ed. I. Douglas-Wilson and G. McLachlan. London: Lancet.

Gunji, A. 1996. "Japan." In *International Handbook of Public Health*, ed. K. Hurrelmann and U. Laaser. London: Greenwood Press.

Linhart, Sepp. 1984. "The Family as a Constitutive Element of Japanese Civilization." In *Senri Ethnological Studies* 16:51–58.

MaloneBeach, E.; Zarit, S.; and Spore, D. 1992. "Caregivers' Perception of Case Management and Community-based Services: Barriers to Service Use." In *Journal of Applied Gerontology* 11 (June): 146–59.

Ministry of Health. 1998. Health Services Planning Department. Web site, home page, March.

Raffel, M. 1984. "Health Services in the United States of America." In *Comparative Health Systems: Descriptive Analyses of Fourteen National Health Systems*. University Park: Pennsylvania State University Press.

Rubin, H.; Owens, A.; and Golden, G. 1998. *Status Report: An Investigation to Determine Whether the Built Environment Affects Patients' Medical Outcomes*. Martinez, Calif.: Center for Health Design.

Seidl, F.; Applebaum, R.; Austin, C.; and Mahoney, K. 1983. *Delivering In-Home Services to the Aged and Disabled*. Lexington, Ky.: D. C. Heath.

Thompson, J., and Goldin, G. 1975. *The Hospital: A Social and Architectural History*. New Haven, Conn.: Yale University Press.

Ulrich, R. 1984. "View through a Window May Influence Recovery from Surgery." In *Science* 224:420–21.

———. 1991. "Effects of Interior Design on Wellness: Theory and Recent Scientific Research." In *Journal of Health Care Interior Design* 3:97–109.

U.S. Bureau of the Census. 1997. *Statistical Abstracts of the United States: 1997*. 117th ed. Washington, D.C.: Government Printing Office.

USDHHS (U.S. Department of Health and Human Services). 1997. *Health, United States, 1996–97: An Injury Chartbook*. Hyattsville, Md.: U.S. Department of Health and Human Services, National Center for Health Statistics.

SIX

Don't Forget Us! Gender Roles in Japanese Civics Textbooks

KYOKO MURAKAMI

Since the Decade of Women,[1] a growing awareness of the need for "balancing" educational materials to improve the coverage and treatment of gender roles has become visible in Japan. "Gender" is a culturally and socially shaped attribute that leads to expected behavior patterns of males and females (Carelli 1988; Measor and Sikes 1992). To investigate whether there is a gender bias in educational materials, a number of studies have examined gender-related language and illustrations in textbooks as well as the curricular content of textbooks. Although current textbooks tend to be more "balanced" than previous editions, gender discrepancy in textbooks is still prevalent, particularly in the context of the labor force (Fukutomi and Saitō 1985; Higuchi et al. 1994; Itō 1991a, 1991b; Kamiko 1991b; Kurata 1987; Sakaki 1986; Yamada et al. 1994; Yoshioka 1991a, 1991b).

A number of articles have suggested that Japanese textbooks reflect a male-dominated outlook. Japanese textbooks, for instance, have depicted female adults and children as sensitive, dependent, less intelligent, and weak compared to their male counterparts (Itō 1991a, 1991b, 1991c, 1991d; Hiruta et al. 1994; Kamiko 1991a; Morimoto 1998; Murata 1994; Sakaki 1986). Supporting traditional gender roles, Japanese textbooks suggested that women's primary roles included household management and child care (Itō 1991b, 1991d; Kamiko 1991a; Morimoto 1998; Murata 1994; Sakaki 1986). The emphasis on traditional female roles

---

[1] In the 1975 International Women's Year, the UN General Assembly held the 1975 World Conference in Mexico. As a result of this conference, the General Assembly adopted the proclamation of a United Nations Decade for Women with the themes equality, development, and peace.

severely limits the occurrences of women portrayed as central figures or decision makers, especially in regard to the labor force (Fukutomi and Saitō 1985; Itō 1991a, 1991b, 1991d; Kurata 1987; Yoshioka 1991a).

Past research has shown that textbooks have significant ideological and political influence in Japan (Cogan and Weber 1983; Cogan and Enloe 1987; Dore 1970; Horio 1988). Notably, education laws in Japan require that the Ministry of Education approve all textbooks for use in both public and private schools (grades 1–12). The laws also specify textbooks as the primary source for classroom instruction. Therefore, textbooks are practically "the only tool for teaching and learning" in Japan (Tani et al. 1993:70). Consequently, textbooks were selected for examination because they play a paramount role in embedding and perpetuating educational polices that affect the role of women in the labor force.

Although recent studies of Japanese textbooks concerning gender have made important contributions, little empirical study exists that explains to what extent and in what manner educational policies have marginalized female roles in the labor force. To address this gap in the literature, this study employs latent content analysis to examine the coverage and treatment of gender in the labor force in civics textbooks. It focuses specifically on whether there are gender biases in Japanese textbooks. It defines "gender biases" as the assumptions and understandings that one sex or one type of gender-role is superior to another in the context of social and economic standards (Carelli 1988).

Method

This study employs latent content analysis to examine the coverage and treatment of gender roles in the labor force in civics textbooks used in junior high schools between 1981 and 1997. Latent content analysis, known as "qualitative" analysis, seeks to identify the contextual or concealed meanings that may be embedded in the medium. Latent analysis presents detailed descriptions of the phenomenon in the form of narrative. This systematic and replicable technique is used to facilitate other scholars' use of the data and procedure for comparison or further development (Holsti 1969; Krippendorff 1980; Weber 1985).

Latent content analysis in this study examines the discourse surrounding the discussions of gender roles in the labor force that appear in written texts. This study attempts to determine whether gender roles in the labor force have been treated in an inappropriate manner as defined later in the coding categories.

Sample

The sample consists of sixteen civics textbooks used in junior high schools in Japan between 1981 and 1997 that have been authorized by the Ministry of Education (1981, 1987, 1993, 1997; see reference list). Among the school subject areas, civics is the key subject that deals with the conditions and problems of women in the labor force in Japan. The textbooks sampled in this study are widely used in Japan. They have been adopted in more than 90 percent of junior high schools since 1981. Furthermore, all Japanese junior high school students must take civics to fulfill the requirements for compulsory education.

Latent Content Analysis Coding Procedure

The coding procedure used in this study consisted of four basic steps. The first step was to develop a recording sheet (copies of the latent analysis coding sheets are available on request). This study examines any word, sentence, or paragraph that depicts gender roles in the labor force in an inappropriate or impertinent manner. Illustrations and photographs are not considered in this study. For this study, a recording sheet was designed to record occurrences of "inappropriate" treatment of gender roles in the labor force as defined by the following categories: distortion, reaction, obscurity, or marginalization. The second step involved establishing a set of latent analysis coding rules (a copy of the latent analysis coding rules is available on request). These detailed rules served as a direction for both me and the independent coders who conducted a reliability check on a sample of textbooks. Pretesting both the recording sheet and the coding rules to ensure the analytic concerns of the study and to minimize the arbitrary interpretation and misunderstanding of the directions was the third step. After several trials and revisions of the recording sheets and coding rules, intercoder reliability checks were conducted. The final step involved the actual coding of the data in the recording sheets. Each page of the textbooks was checked carefully to obtain accurate data.

Coding Categories

The coding categories established in this study are based on the classification of an inappropriate treatment of gender roles in the labor force. A sentence or paragraph was recorded in its entirety if it fit into any of the following categories: distortion, reaction, obscurity, or marginalization.

Distortion	Text that falsely and improperly depicts gender roles in the labor force.
Reaction	Text that emphasizes traditional gender roles as a fundamental value, or places little importance on female roles in the labor force.
Obscurity	Text that is ambiguous or that conceals gender-related problems in the labor force.
Marginalization	Text that treats gender roles in the labor force as peripheral or even outside the realm of main contents.

Reliability and Validity of the Study

Reliability checks of the latent analyses were addressed through the use of intercoder reliability checks. This procedure obtained a consensus achieved among other coders toward the targeted sample of the textbooks. The intercoder reliability checks were completed after I had coded a subsample of four textbooks. A subsample of textbooks was selected for every published year, one textbook per year, in accordance with the alphabetical order of the publishers. Two coders who are native speakers of Japanese were independently assigned to code a word, sentence, or paragraph related to gender roles in the labor force. Intercoder reliability was obtained by Scott's (1955) *pi* index. An assessment of the intercoder reliability between two coders and me in this study was .81. These results were an acceptable range; content analyses typically report a minimum reliability above .75 (Scott).

Validity checks are also important in content analysis. Validity refers to the extent to which the results or design of the study actually measures the realities of the world. To assess the validity, this study employed content validity. Content validity, also known as face validity, has frequently been used in content analysis (Holsti 1969; Weber 1985). It is accomplished by citing some of the content that appears in Japanese civics textbooks directly to demonstrate the accuracy of content definition and its measurement (Holsti 1969). Considering the circumstances, many questions have been left unanswered regarding Japanese women in the labor force. This study attempts to answer some of the unexplored questions.

Results and Discussion

The results of the latent content analysis of the sixteen textbooks showed many instances where gender roles in the labor force have been treated in an improper manner as defined by the categories distortion, reaction, obscurity, and marginalization.

Distortion

This study defined the term "distortion" as text that falsely and improperly depicts gender roles in the labor force. Two instances conforming to this definition appeared in the sampled textbooks. The first example of distortion appeared in Kikuchi et al.'s civics textbook (1987). The text suggested that the increase in the numbers of both parents working outside the home has caused an increase in domestic tragedies such as suicides or divorces. The textbook stated:

> The number of dual-income families is increasing. Family life is also changing in these ways: parents leave their children in day-care centers, eat out for their meals, or buy ready-made meals.... Within this transition, dismal incidents such as serious family tragedies due to conflicts between parents and children or family suicides have been reported. A rapid increase of divorce has caused many problems in raising children. Also, there is the problem of supporting elderly people. (p. 16; my translation)

By ignoring other factors (e.g., labor problems, violence in media, or gender discrimination in Japanese society) that can cause the social problems noted above, this textbook was sending the message that these social problems are caused by straying from traditional family roles, specifically the traditional roles of the female such as staying at home, nursing her children, and preparing meals for the family. In a similar but even more deliberate manner, several other textbooks suggested that many social problems occurred because of "the transition of fundamental family roles" from traditional gender roles to more balanced gender roles.

Another example of distorting gender roles in the labor force appeared in Takayanagi et al.'s textbook (1997). This textbook suggested that women are less efficient in managing both a job and household tasks than men are. The textbook stated:

> Women have been treated unfairly in various stages regarding recruitment, employment, assignment, and promotion. It is mainly that women cannot manage both their jobs and household tasks, nursing their children and the elderly. The great need is to improve labor conditions as a whole and to initiate birth and child-care leaves or a full day-care center for workers of both sexes. (p. 30, my translation)

Although the authors of the textbook acknowledged the unfair treatment of Japanese women in the labor force, they emphasized a woman's inability to successfully maintain a full time job in addition to taking care of her family. Simultaneously, the textbook failed to mention that while women struggle to maintain both career and domestic responsibilities, their male counterparts remain free from almost all domestic tasks. It could be difficult for junior high school students to understand the problems of female workers without mentioning the oppression of women in both family and in the labor force.

In 1993, a survey in metropolitan Tokyo showed that almost all (approximately 98 percent) of the housekeeping (e.g., cooking, cleaning, washing, and caring for children and aged parents) was done by women, except tutoring children's studies (cited in Keizai kikaku-chō 1997:85). This disproportionate figure does not change when women work full time. In 1990, for instance, women performed 90.4 percent of the household tasks (Rōdō-shō 1992: 149). This reality reflects the huge gap between the sexes concerning household responsibilities. While more than half of Japan's wives desire to have jobs and to share household responsibilities with their spouses, more than half of Japanese husbands avoid the household responsibilities even when both wife and husband are in the labor force (Keizai kikaku-chō 1997:84). In ignoring this situation, the textbook did not refer to the core of the matter.

Reaction

The term "reaction" was operationally defined as a text that emphasizes traditional gender roles as a fundamental value or places little importance on female roles in the labor force. Civics textbooks frequently treated gender roles in the labor force in a reactionary manner. In most instances, however, the textbooks did not directly state that women should stay in their traditional roles. Rather, the textbooks subtly suggested that women should be allowed to work only after they fulfill their household duties, nurse their children, and take care of their aged parents. For instance, Ukai et al. (1981) cited an opinion poll that asked female workers what concerns they have when pursuing their jobs. The results of the poll explained that most of the concerns for female workers were related to domestic duties and caring for their children. The authors commented that "they understood how difficult it is for female workers to manage both work and household tasks" (p. 181). These textbooks promoted the assumption that women were the only ones who need to manage domestic and child-rearing responsibilities in addition to their jobs.

Though many textbooks acknowledged an increase of women in the labor force, some textbooks characterized men as the sole breadwinners of their families and women as dependents. These textbooks are sending the hidden message that men's primary responsibility is to work for a living in the labor force while women's primary responsibility is to maintain the household. In other words, the textbooks suggested that performing household responsibilities are secondary duties for men and that making a living is not the primary responsibility for women. An example appeared in Takayanagi et al.'s textbook. It stated:

> At present, because each individual has his or her own interests, wives and husbands or parents and children tend to have fewer opportunities to understand each other. Household duties and raising children have been the responsibilities of the wives. Husbands are so tied up in their work that they have no time to think of their families. (1987, p. 212; my translation)

Reasoning that husbands are too busy to think about their families because of their demanding jobs, textbooks suggest, in a roundabout manner, that traditional gender roles are necessary for society. In a similar manner, two textbooks characterized men as breadwinners by using phrases such as "fatherless family that lost the breadwinner in their families" (Satō, Nomura, and Kitajima 1981:180; Kawata, Bitō, and Yamaka 1987:26).

Empathizing with the special protection of women is another form of reaction. According to the Ministry of Labor (cited in Nippon Fujin dantai rengō-kai, 1996), the top three reasons why companies hire only male workers are that (1) some duties, such as late-night shifts and carrying heavy materials violate the special protection of women enforced by the Labor Standards Law (38.1 percent); (2) women lack the necessary qualification or skill for pursuing their duties (35 percent); and (3) there is a significant amount of overtime work (27.8 percent). Interestingly, almost all textbooks referred to the special protection of women (15 textbooks) as a positive feature of the law; however, none of them further discussed how this special protection promoted discrimination against female workers.[2] By mentioning the special protection of women without any further discussion, Japanese textbooks suggest that female workers would not be equal partners because women need protection.

Obscurity

Of the four inappropriate treatment categories, "obscurity" appeared the most in the sampled Japanese civics textbooks. The term "obscurity" was operationally defined as a text that is ambiguous or conceals sex discrimination in the labor force. For example, if a textbook recognizes sex discrimination in the labor force but does not provide any concrete examples of the problem or introduces a term or concept that hides the inner meaning of the phenomenon, the text was classified as "obscure."

Although many textbooks recognized sex discrimination in the labor force, possible solutions or explanations of why it exist are treated obscurely. In suggesting ways to eliminate all forms of sex discrimination including unequal employment opportunity and treatment, the majority of textbooks made ambiguous moral or somewhat sentimental suggestions. Examples of these suggestions include the effort to eliminate sex discrimination (10 textbooks), women's self-awareness (6 textbooks), or men's understanding (4 textbooks). These examples typically appeared as follows:

> To establish equality for both men and women, political power is necessary, but the most important thing is a woman's self-awareness and a man's understanding. (Kawata, Bitō, and Tanabe 1993:55; my translation)

> The Japanese constitution is based on the idea that each individual should be fully respected regardless of his or her sex. It is harmful to maintain individual dignity if society restricts social roles because you are a man or woman. We would like to create an affluent society in which independent men and women accept each other's personalities. (Satō et al., 1997:47; my translation)

---

[2] All provisions related to the special protection of women were canceled by April 1999 in accordance with the 1997 Equal Employment Opportunity Law (EEOL) reform (see Takahashi 1998 and Takenaka 1998 for details).

The content of the textbooks by Kawata, Bitō, and Tanabe or Satō et al. that I studied brings up many interesting questions. What kinds of efforts can we make to help eliminate sex discrimination? What does women's self-awareness mean? To what extent should men understand gender roles in the labor force and how? What do men and women's responsibilities mean? There is no definite answer to such questions. Although textbooks acknowledge the existence of sex discrimination in the labor force, they don't explain why women are discriminated against. Out of four textbooks, only two reasons were provided: the biological reason, namely, childbirth (1 textbook); and fewer years of service (3 textbooks). As I noted in the "reaction" section, these reasons do not address the main point of the issue.

Another form of obscurity, which appeared in four textbooks, suggested that the enactment of the EEOL, which guarantees equal opportunity for and equal treatment of both sexes, was welfare for female workers rather than a fundamental human right. One example stated:

> In the fields of the labor force, the government will take action to promote welfare for female workers to ensure equal employment opportunities and equal treatment for both men and women. (Kikuchi et al., 1987:135; my translation)

Welfare is, by definition, provided by the government. However, allowing individuals to fully develop their personality and talents without discrimination because of their sex is a fundamental human right. These types of obscure explanations in Japanese civics textbooks may confuse both female and male children.

Recently, Japan has instituted the Child-Care Leave Law and Adult-Care Absence Law for both female and male workers. The theoretical framework of these laws is based on equal participation of men and women in household management and raising children as well as in caring for aged parents. Nevertheless, Satō et al.'s textbook provides an ambiguous message; some readers might misinterpret the systems for child-care leave and adult-care leave as meant only for women. They state:

> In Japan, we are making an effort to eliminate discrimination between men and women in the work place such as recruitment, employment, promotion, retirement, and dismissal by enforcing the Equal Employment Opportunity Law for men and women since 1986. There are problems of re-employment of women and expansion of systems for child-care leave and adult-care leave. (1997:130; my translation)

To avoid any kind of misinterpretation, textbooks should provide a clear explanation concerning the significance of the laws to the students.

The final instance of obscurity appeared in eleven of the textbooks; it shows a substantive pattern of improper treatment of gender roles in the labor force. This prevalent obscurity consisted of omitting the important contribution of women as productive workers throughout the centuries. For example:

> Once there was an assumption that men should be in the workplace and women should be at home (gender roles). Recently, however, more females in the labor force have been required for the society.... These days in Japan, approximately half of women who are older than fifteen years old are committed to their occupation. (Takayanagi et al., 1987:52; my translation)

Because of these obscure treatments of the subject matter, some students may misinterpret the text as implying that women were never engaged in work other than household tasks and raising their children and caring for elderly members of their families. Throughout the twentieth century, more than half of the Japanese women have been in the labor force as self-employed workers, family workers, or so-called employees (Kumazawa 1996). Since the 1950s, women have made up approximately 40 percent of the labor force (Rōdō-shō 1998). The typical gender roles referred to in the previous quotation confuse the issue.

Marginalization

The term "marginalization" was operationally defined as gender roles in the labor force being treated as peripheral or even outside the realm of the main contents. Japanese textbooks commonly marginalize the issues around sex discrimination in the labor force. For instance, they have printed the subject matter in a smaller font size within the main text or in areas isolated from the main text such as "reference" or "discussion box" sections.

The marginalization of sex discrimination in the labor force takes a variety of faces. Although many textbooks have recognized the problems of such discrimination in the labor force, Japanese textbooks marginalize the discrepancy between laws and realities. For example, the Labor Standards Law of Japan adopted the principle of equal wages for female and male workers in 1947; however, only three textbooks mentioned this fact. Two out of the three instances appearing in the main text had a smaller font size, and the principle of equal wages for female and male workers was not discussed in any detail. None of the textbooks mentions it in relation to the crucial reality of the wage discrimination against female workers. In 1997, for instance, the actual monthly earnings of women were only 51 percent of their male counterparts' earnings.[3]

Another issue in which sex discrimination in the labor force was marginalized was in the lack of discussion about government policies. Though a number of academic and nonacademic articles have questioned the practical effect of the EEOL (e.g., Kodera 1994; Koike 1996; Kumazawa 1996; Molony 1995; Takenaka 1998; Wakisaka 1997), this study found only four passages that pointed out such questions. Furthermore, two out of the four appeared in an isolated area of a textbook. In other words, Japanese textbooks avoid highlighting the issues of gender roles and sex discrimination in the labor force.

Conclusion

This study examined the coverage and treatment of gender roles in the labor force in sixteen Japanese civics textbooks used in junior high school between 1981 and 1997 to discover whether or not there were gender biases in Japanese textbooks. "Gender biases" were defined as assumptions or understandings that one sex or one type of gender role is superior to the other in the context of social and economic standards (Carelli 1988). To help answer the question, latent content analysis developed coding categories based on the classification of an inappropriate or inapt treatment of gender roles in the labor force such as distortion, reaction, obscurity, or marginalization.

Based on this study, two generalizations can be suggested. First, textbooks seem to acknowledge that men and women should share household tasks and that women should participate in the labor force. However, textbooks also support the assumption that women's primary roles are household management, raising their children, and caring for elderly family members. Curricular perspectives concerning women seem to promote and perpetuate a cultural and historical burden of gender roles. Such "slanting" has been accomplished by distorting, reacting, concealing, or

---

[3] This included part-time workers. Full-time female workers earn approximately 61 percent of what their male counterparts earn (Rōdō-shō, cited in Nippon fujin dantai rengō-kai 1998:286).

marginalizing the important issues in texts concerning gender roles in the labor force. Supporting traditional gender roles, Japanese textbooks have strongly discouraged female students from pursuing their professional careers.

Second, Japanese children seldom receive any comprehensive explanation regarding the rights of women to work without discrimination. Although textbooks provided much factual information about existing sex discrimination in the labor force, none of the textbooks explained why it happened or what it was like to be involved in a case of discrimination. Such oversights were particularly obvious when the information provided in the textbooks involved anything of political significance such as special protection provisions for women, insufficient reform of the EEOL, or the principle of equal wages for female and male workers. Many textbooks did not address the important issues that are the core of gender-role problems in the labor force, instead concealing, marginalizing, and reacting to these issues. Both female and male junior high school students in Japan might have difficulty fully understanding the target issues.

Finally, given the "slanted" contents concerning gender roles in Japanese textbooks and the concealment of significant background information on sex discrimination in the labor force, junior high school students who use these textbooks may unwittingly come to accept assumptions and behaviors that are socially and culturally embedded. In other words, Japanese textbooks contribute to the promotion of the status quo.

The results of the latent analysis indicate that many instances of gender roles and sex discrimination in the labor force in Japanese civics textbooks were superficial and misleading. Various findings of this study also supported earlier findings of sex discrimination or "slanted" descriptions of gender roles based on the idea that attributes and functions frequently assigned to the feminine role are less highly regarded than those attributed to the masculine role. As a result, women are described as passive experts in household and child-care duties while men are portrayed as active agents in the labor force (Fukutomi and Saitō 1985; Higuchi et al. 1994; Itō 1991a, 1991b, 1991c, 1991d; Kamiko 1991a, 1991b; Kurata 1987; Morimoto 1998; Murata 1994; Sakaki 1986; Yamada et al. 1994; Yoshioka 1991a, 1991b).

One may assume that a curricular content regarding gender roles in textbooks reflects the existing realities in the labor force. This attitude poses a problem, however, because there is no rational explanation for textbook support of sex discrimination in the labor force. If textbook writers do not make an effort to improve the content of textbooks concerning sex discrimination and gender roles in the labor force, they perpetuate and reinforce the realities of discrimination in the name of education. Female students may be less likely to pursue professional careers. There is no justification for such perpetuation. Textbooks should not merely be concerned with existing realities that are culturally and historically embedded in society. Rather, they should provide an education based on the concept of equal education corresponding to ability, not sex. This basic educational policy is prescribed in the Japanese constitution as well as by the Education Law in Japan.

To summarize, this study found that there is much inappropriate treatment of gender roles in the labor force in Japanese textbooks. It is recommended that the knowledge and information obtained by this study be used by educators as well as policy makers to improve the textbook contents concerning such matters.

References

Carelli, A. O. 1988. Introduction. In *Sex Equity in Education,* ed. A. O. Carelli, xi–xxv. Springfield, Ill.: Charles C. Thomas.

Cogan, J. J., and R. E. Weber. 1983. "The Japanese History Textbook Controversy and What We Can Learn from It." *Social Education* 47(4):253–56.

Cogan, J. J., and W. Enloe. 1987. "The Japanese History Textbook Controversy Revisited." *Social Education* 51(10):450–54.

Dore, R. P. 1987. "Notes and Comment: Textbook Censorship in Japan—the Ienaga Case." *Pacific Affairs* 43:548–56.

Fukutomi Mamoru and Mie Saitō. 1985. "Shōgakkō Kyōkasho niokeru Seiyakuwari no Bunseki" (An analysis of sex roles in elementary school textbooks). *Bulletin of Tokyo Gakugei University Sect. I* 36:59–69.

Higuchi Keiko, Ikuko Nakagawa, Junko Uchida, Yūko Tanaka, Mieko Kamimoto, Shizuko Yanagi, Keiko Suga, and Tomiko Matsumura. 1994. "Shakai Kyōkasho no bunseki" (An analysis of social science textbooks). In *Shōgakkō Zen-kyōkasho no Bunseki* (Analyses of all textbooks in elementary school levels), ed. 21-seiki Kyōiku Mondai Kenkyūkai, 94–116. Tokyo: Rōdō Kyōiku Sentā.

72 Kyōko Murakami

Hiruta Junko, Hiroko Kobayashi, and Kanagawa-ken 21-seiki Kyōiku Mondai Kenkyūkai Kaiin. 1994. "Kokugo Kyōkasho no bunseki" (An analysis of Japanese-language textbooks). In *Shōgakkō Zen-kyōkasho no Bunseki* (Analyses of all textbooks in elementary school levels), ed. 21-seiki Kyōiku Mondai Kenkyūkai, 27–93. Tokyo: Rōdō Kyōiku Sentā.

Holsti, Ole. 1969. *Content Analysis for the Social Sciences and Humanities.* Reading, Mass.: Addison-Wesley.

Horio, T. 1988. *Educational Thought and Ideology in Modern Japan.* Ed. and trans. S. Platzer. Tokyo: University of Tokyo Press.

Itō Yoshinori. 1991a. "Shōgakkō Kyōkasho no Genjō: Kokugo" (Japanese language textbooks in elementary school levels). In *Kyōkasho no Naka no Danjosabetsu* (Gender discrimination in textbooks), 15–43. Tokyo: Akashi Shoten.

———. 1991b. "Shōgakkō Kyōkasho no Genjō: Dōtoku" (Moral education textbooks in elementary school levels). In *Kyōkasho no Naka no Danjosabetsu* (Gender discrimination in textbooks), 88–122. Tokyo: Akashi Shoten.

———. 1991c. "Chūgakkō Kyōkasho no Genjō: Kokugo" (Japanese language textbooks in junior high school levels). In *Kyōkasho no Naka no Danjosabetsu* (Gender discrimination in textbooks), 125–45. Tokyo: Akashi Shoten.

———. 1991d. "Chūgakkō Kyōkasho no Genjō: Dōtoku" (Moral education textbooks in junior high school levels). In *Kyōkasho no Naka no Danjosabetsu* (Gender discrimination in textbooks), 185–210. Tokyo: Akashi Shoten.

Kamiko Tatsuko. 1991a. "Shōgakkō Kyōkasho no Genjō: Kateika" (Home economics textbooks in elementary school levels). In *Kyōkasho no Naka no Danjosabetsu* (Gender discrimination in textbooks), 59–87. Tokyo: Akashi Shoten.

———. 1991b. "Chūgakkō Kyōkasho no Genjō: Gijutsu Katei" (Home engineering and home economics textbooks in junior high school levels). In *Kyōkasho no Naka no Danjosabetsu* (Gender discrimination in textbooks), 173–84. Tokyo: Akashi Shoten.

Keizai Kikaku-chō, ed. 1997. *Kokumin Seikatsu Hakusho* (National life white paper). Tokyo: Ōkura-shō.

Kodera, Kyōko. 1994. "The Reality of Equality for Japanese Female Workers: Women's Careers within Japanese Style of Management." *Social Justice* 21(56):136–54.

Koike, Kazuo. 1996. *The Economics of Work in Japan.* Tokyo: LTCB International Library Foundation.

Krippendorff, Kraus. 1980. *Content Analysis: An Introduction to Its Methodology.* Beverly Hills, Calif.: Sage.

Kumazawa, Makoto. 1996. *Portraits of the Japanese Workplace: Labor Movements, Workers, and Managers.* Ed. A. Gordon. Trans. M. Hane. Boulder, Colo.: Westview Press.

Kurata Kanji. 1987. "Seisa no Mondai" (Problems of sex differences). In *Kyōkasho no Shakaigakuteki Kenkyū* (Social scientific studies on textbooks), ed. Tokuo Kataoka, 98–115. Tokyo: Fukumura Shuppan.

Measor, Linda, and Patricia Sikes. 1992. *Gender and Schools.* New York: Cassell.

Molony, Barbara. 1995. "Japan's 1986 Equal Employment Opportunity Law and the Changing Discourse on Gender." *Signs* 20(2):268–302.

Morimoto Eriko. 1998. "Jenda o Saiseisan suru Bungaku Kyōzai" (Gender reproducing in narrative teaching materials). *Women's Studies* 6:30–45.

Murata Yasuhiko. 1994. "Kyōkasho Bunseki no Shiten" (Viewpoints of textbook analyses). In *Shōgakkō Zen-kyōkasho no Bunseki* (Analyses of all textbooks in elementary school levels), ed. 21-seiki Kyōiku Mondai Kenkyūkai Tokyo, 18–26. Rōdō Kyōiku Sentā.

Nippon Fujin Dantai Rengō-kai, ed. 1996. *Fujin Hakusho* (Women's white paper). Tokyo: Horupu Shuppan.

Rōdō-shō, ed. 1992. *Rōdō Hakusho* (Labor white paper). Tokyo: Nippon Rōdō Kenkyū Kikō.

———. 1998. *Rōdō Hakusho* (Labor white paper). Tokyo: Nippon Rōdō Kenkyū Kikō.

Sakai Harumi. 1995. *Kyōkasho ga Kaita Kazoku to Josei no Sengo 50-nen* (Family and women in textbooks over the fifty years of the postwar period). Tokyo: Rōdō Kyōiku Sentā.

Sakaki Kyōko. 1986. "Shōgakkō Kyōkasho no nakani Miru Danjo Sabetsu (Sex discrimination in elementary school textbooks). *Kaiho Kyōiku* 204:40–54.

Scott, William A. 1955. "Reliability of Content Analysis: The Case of Nominal Scale Coding." *Public Opinion Quarterly* 17:321–25.

Takahashi, Hiroyuki. 1998. "Working Women in Japan: A Look at Historical Trends and Legal Reform." Japan Economic Institute Report, 42A (November 6): 1–10.

Takenaka Emiko. 1998. "Rōdōbunya niokeru Kiseikanwa to Josei Seisaku" (Deregulation and policies concerning women in the labor field). *Women's Studies Review* 6:27–46.

Tani, Masaru, et al. 1993. "Textbook Development and Selection in Japan and the United States." *Social Education* 57(2):70–75.

Wakisaka, Akira. 1997. "Women at Work." In *Japanese Labour and Management in Transition*, ed. M. Sako and H. Satō, 131–50. London: Routledge.

Weber, R. P. 1985. *Basic Content Analysis*. Beverly Hills, Calif.: Sage.

Wimmer, R. D., and J. R. Dominick. 1994. *Mass Media Research: An Introduction*. 4th ed. Belmont, Calif.: Wadsworth.

Yamada Mutsuko, Junko Naitō, and Hokkaidō 21-seiki Kyōiku Mondai Kenkyūkai Kaiin. 1994. "Katei Kyōkasho no bunseki" (An analysis of home economics textbooks). In *Shōgakkō Zenkyōkasho no Bunseki* (Analyses of all textbooks in elementary school levels), ed. 21-seiki Kyōiku Mondai Kenkyūkai Tokyo, 200–9. Tokyo: Rōdō Kyōiku Sentā.

Yoshioka Mutsuko. 1991a. "Shōgakkō Kyōkasho no Genjō: Shakaika" (Social science textbooks in elementary school levels). In *Kyōkasho no Naka no Danjosabetsu* (Gender discrimination in textbooks), 44–58. Tokyo: Akashi Shoten.

———. 1991b. "Chūgakkō Kyōkasho no Genjō: Shakaika Rekishiteki Bunya" (Social science–history textbooks in junior high school level). In *Kyōkasho no Naka no Danjosabetsu* (Gender discrimination in textbooks), 146–56. Tokyo: Akashi Shoten.

———. 1991c. "Chūgakkō Kyōkasho no Genjō: Shakaika Kōminteki Bunya" (Junior high school social science–civics textbooks). In *Kyōkasho no Naka no Danjosabetsu* (Gender discrimination in textbooks), 157–72. Tokyo: Akashi Shoten.

Sampled Textbooks

Horio Teruhisa et al. 1997. *Chūgaku Shakai: Kōminteki Bunya* (Social science in junior high schools: Civics). Tokyo: Nihon Shoseki.

Kawata Tsuyoshi, Masahide Bitō, and Seiji Yamaka, eds. 1987. *Atarashii Shakai: Kōmin* (New social science: Civics). Tokyo: Tōkyō Shoseki.

Kawata Tsuyoshi, Masahide Bitō, and Yū Tanabe, eds. 1993. *Atarashii Shakai: Kōmin* (New social science: Civics). Tokyo: Tōkyō Shoseki.

Kihara Kentaro et al. 1981. *Chūgaku Shakai: Kōminteki Bunya* (Social science in junior high schools: Civics). Osaka: Ōsaka Shoseki.

Kikuchi Isamu et al. 1987. *Chūgaku Shakai: Kōminteki Bunya* (Social science in junior high schools: Civics). Osaka: Ōsaka Shoseki.

Kōno Shigeo, Jiku Satō, and Masakazu Nomura, eds. 1987. *Chūgaku Shakai: Kōminteki Bunya* (Social science in junior high schools: Civics). Tokyo: Kyōiku Shuppan.

Kōno Shigeo, Jiku Satō, Yoshio Okuda, and Haruo Sasayama, eds. 1993. *Chūgaku Shakai: Kōminteki Bunya* (Social science in junior high schools: Civics). Tokyo: Kyōiku Shuppan.

———. 1997. *Chūgaku Shakai: Kōminteki Bunya* (Social science in junior high schools: Civics). Tokyo: Kyōiku Shuppan.

Ozaki Morimitsu et al. 1981. *Chūgaku Shakai: Kōminteki Bunya* (Social science in junior high schools: Civics). Tokyo: Nihon Shoseki.

Satō Jiku, Masakazu Nomura, and Masamoto Kitajima, eds. 1981. *Chūgaku Shakai: Kōminteki Bunya* (Social science in junior high schools: Civics). Tokyo: Kyōiku Shuppan.

Satō Koji et al. 1993. *Chūgaku Shakai: Kōminteki Bunya* (Social science in junior high schools: Civics). Osaka: Ōsaka Shoseki.

———. 1997. *Chūgaku Shakai: Kōminteki Bunya* (Social science in junior high schools: Civics). Osaka: Ōsaka Shoseki.

Takayanagi Shinichi et al. 1987. *Chūgaku Shakai: Kōminteki Bunya* (Social science in junior high schools: Civics). Tokyo: Nihon Shoseki.

———. 1993. *Chūgaku Shakai: Kōminteki Bunya* (Social science in junior high schools: Civics). Tokyo: Nihon Shoseki.

Tanabe Yū, Takashi Yoshida, and Nobuo Sakagami, eds. 1997. *Atarashii Shakai: Kōmin* (New social science: Civics). Tokyo: Tōkyō Shoseki.

Ukai Nobunari, Tsuyoshi Kawata, Masahide Bitō, and Seiji Yamaka, eds. 1981. *Atarashii Shakai: Kōmin* (New social science: Civics). Tokyo: Tōkyō Shoseki.

SEVEN

Linguistic Creativity: Pseudo-borrowing in Japanese Writing

SHOJI AZUMA

Modern Japanese is characterized by a heavy influx of linguistic borrowings, mostly from English. According to Honna (1995), 13 percent of the vocabulary used in daily conversation consists of loan words. Furthermore, 60–70 percent of new words in the dictionaries of neologisms are from English. The heavy influx of loan words has stimulated research on their forms and functions (Azuma 1997a, b; Haarmann 1984; Hayashi and Hayashi 1995; Honna 1995; Iwasaki 1994; Kay 1995; Loveday 1986, 1996; Miyaji 1990; Morrow 1987; Ono 1992; Stanlow 1987; Takashi 1990). In addition to "cultural borrowings" that fill a lexical gap, there are also "core borrowings" that function not merely as lexical filler (Myers-Scotton 1992, 1993). Research on linguistic borrowing in Japanese has shown that it can convey the image of modernity, sophistication, and internationalization because of the symbolic value of English as an international language (e.g., Haarmann 1984; Takashi 1990). In addition, borrowing is shown to function as a way to negotiate interpersonal relations between a speaker and a listener in a given discourse (e.g., Azuma 1997a; Hayashi and Hayashi 1995).

This study extends the research on borrowing and shows that in Japan, contact with other languages in Japan has resulted in an innovative mechanism of borrowing that has not been researched thoroughly. That is, native Japanese words are being treated in writing as if they were borrowings. Writing native Japanese words with the same orthographic system (*katakana*) used for "real" borrowings creates a new set of "pseudo-borrowings." In this chapter, I will examine various pseudo-borrowings and show that they can function as a discourse strategy along the lines of

Brown and Levinson's politeness theory. First, however, a brief introduction of the Japanese writing system is in order.

The Japanese Writing System

Unlike languages such as English, Japanese uses three writing systems, each of which has its own distinctive function. *Kanji* (logograms or Chinese characters) are used for Sino-Japanese words (loan words of Chinese origin) or content words (e.g., nouns, verb stems). *Hiragana* (rounded syllabic script), which came about by simplifying the grass (i.e., cursive) style of writing characters, is used for native grammatical words or function words (e.g., inflection, post position). *Katakana* (angular syllabic script), developed as abbreviations of characters, is used for foreign words (other than those of Chinese origin) and onomatopoeia (Shibatani 1990). Because each of the three writing systems has its own separate functions, they are often used in the same sentence. Observe the following examples.[1]

1.

bitamin	wa	karada	no	junkatsuyu		desu
vitamin	TOP	body	GEN	lubricating oil		is

Vitamins are the lubricating oil for the body.

2.

chuukan	tesuto	no	puresshaa	ga	tsuyo-katta
middle	test	GEN	pressure	NOM	strong-was

The pressure from the midterm test was strong.

3.

kinchoo	shi	sugite	shinzoo	ga	dokidoki	suru
tension	become	exceed	heart	NOM	pound	do

I feel my heart pounding from the high tension.

In (1), *katakana* (e.g., ビタミン), which is a squarish shape, is used for the foreign word "vitamin" (an instance of cultural borrowing). *Hiragana* (e.g., は) is used for function words such as the topic marker. *Kanji* (e.g., 体) is used for content words such as "body." Likewise in (2), *katakana* (e.g., テスト, プレッシャー) is used for foreign words such as "test" and "pressure" (an instance of core borrowing). *Hiragana* is used for function words such as past tense

---

[1] The following abbreviations are used in this study: ACC, accusative; COMP, complimentizer; GEN, genitive; NOM, nominative; Q, question; TAG, tag; TOP, topic.

markers. *Kanji* is used for content words such as noun and verb stems. In (3), *katakana* (e.g., ドキ ドキ) is used for onomatopoeia (here, imitating the sound of heartbeats).

More important than the fact that the three writing systems are visually distinct from each other, they are, in a sense, in complementary distribution in terms of their function. Specifically, *katakana* is reserved for foreign words and onomatopoeia. *Katakana* is not used for native Japanese content words or Sino-Japanese words. *Katakana* is not used for function words either. However, an examination of modern Japanese writing from published materials reveals that the situation is in an unexpected sort of transition. Native speakers of Japanese are extending the use of *katakana* beyond its normal boundaries to native Japanese words. The data for the present study come from the April 12, 1998, issue of *Shuukan Shinchoo* (a weekly magazine) as well as various published materials collected in Japan over a six-month period in 1998.[2]

Katakana Use in Pseudo-borrowings

Katakana, which has been traditionally reserved for foreign words, is now being extended to Japanese words. Observe the following examples in which *katakana* is used in native Japanese words. The italicized portion indicates the use of *katakana*.

4. *Bishi* tto   *kime*ta   *suutsu*   sugata
    sharp COMP   decide   suit   style
    the style of *sharply dressing* in a *suit*

5. *Kakko*   *ii*   otoko   no   *ko*   ni   aeru   kamo-shirenai
    style   good   male   GEN   child   with   meet   may
    (You) may be able to meet a *goodlooking boy.*

Both sentences appear in a magazine aimed at young adults. In (4), *katakana* is used for the onomatopoetic *bishi* 'sharp' and for the foreign word *suutsu* 'suit.' These are environments where we expect to find *katakana*. Interestingly, however, *katakana* is also

---

The following magazines were used for this study: *Asahi Journal,* a weekly magazine; *Bungei Shunju,* a weekly magazine; *Flash,* a weekly magazine; *Nikkei Business,* a weekly economics journal; *Shuukan Bunshun,* a weekly magazine; *Shuukan Hooseki,* a weekly magazine; *Spa,* a weekly magazine; *Tooyoo Keizai,* a weekly economics journal; *Train Vert,* a weekly magazine.

used for the stem *kime* of the verb *kimeta* 'decide' as well. The
verb *kimeta* is in no way foreign, yet *katakana* is used to write it.
In (5), neither the adjective *kakko ii* 'goodlooking' nor the noun *ko*
'child' is a foreign word, but again *katakana* is used to write them.
Those Japanese words could all be easily written in either *hiragana*
or a combination of *hiragana* and *kanji*. This type of borrowing
may be referred to as a pseudo-borrowing, which may be characterized as writing native Japanese words in *katakana* to make them
resemble foreign borrowings.

To determine the relative frequency of pseudo-borrowings in
contemporary Japanese, I examined one issue of the weekly magazine *Shuukan Shinchoo* (April 2, 1998) from cover to cover. The
magazine contained 185 pages. First, I counted all *katakana* words
that appeared in print, then computed the frequency of occurrence
of pseudo-borrowings. There were 3,583 *katakana* words, 252
pseudo-borrowings. The frequency of pseudo-borrowings is relatively small (just 7 percent of all *katakana* words). However, it is
noteworthy that in addition to loan words and onomatopoeia,
Japanese words are also written in *katakana* (i.e., pseudo-
borrowing).

Why would writers decide to choose *katakana* instead of *hiragana* or *kanji* for the Japanese words? *Katakana* is often used to
render coined words (e.g., *charinko* 'bicycle'), because *katakana* is
generally reserved for writing vocabulary that did not exist in the
native Japanese inventory. However, in the magazine studied,
katakana was being used for native Japanese words. What might
be the discourse function of these pseudo-borrowings?

One plausible notion is that the *katakana* writing system works
as an emphasizer or an attention-getter. Observe the following
examples.[3]

6. *Baito*   suru   nara   benri   ga   *ii*
   part time   do   if   convenience   NOM   good
   If (you) work *part time*, a convenient job is *good.*

7. *Gaara*   no-naka-de   ichiban   *muudii*-na   *supotto*
   (ski resort)   at   most   moody   spot
   to   ie   ba   *koko.*
   COMP   say   if   this place
   The most *romantic place* at Gaara is *this place.*

---

[3] The borrowing of *muudii* from English "moody" is an example of semantic
shift. The borrowed form *muudii* is used to mean "romantic atmosphere."

In the above examples, the adjective *ii* 'good' and the noun *koko* 'this place' (as well as borrowed words from English and German) are written in *katakana*. Here the use of *katakana* for Japanese words directs readers' attention to these key words. The squarish shape of *katakana* may well catch the readers' eye. In addition, *katakana* is sometimes used to replace some *kanji* that are difficult or unfamiliar to native speakers of Japanese (e.g., *geta* 'wooden clogs', *kagi* 'key', *goza* 'mat', and *teko* 'lever') (Takebe 1979).

What are some other possible discourse functions of *katakana?* The answer seems to lie in borrowings. Borrowings (mainly from English) are used, as we have noted, to convey an image of modernity, newness, internationality, and sophistication (e.g., Takashi 1990). Writers can use *katakana* for Japanese words to create an effect similar to that caused by foreign borrowings—adding a feel of fashion or sophistication to what they describe. A number of companies use this technique in naming their institutions. Some well-known examples of this are Toyota and Sanyo. However, we also observe this use of *katakana* in various expressions. In examples (5) and (6), Japanese words such as *kakko ii* and *ko* were re-created as pseudo-borrowings. In (5), the word *ko* originally meant "a child." However, by writing it in *katakana* and making it a pseudo-borrowing, *ko* now can refer not merely to a child, but to a young adult who has all characteristics considered desirable among young people. For example, he or she may know the type of music popular among young people or may wear trendy fashions. *Katakana* is used to transform the original Japanese word into someone fashionable or sophisticated.

It is well documented that borrowing is often accompanied by semantic change as well as morphological and phonological change (e.g., Honna 1995; Shibatani 1990). According to Shibatani (1990), the most common type of semantic change is narrowing and specialization, in which only one of several original meanings is retained. For example, the borrowed form *sutoobu*, which comes from English "stove," is used only in the sense of a room heater, never for a cooking stove. The borrowed form *sutekki*, which comes from English "stick," is used only in the sense of a walking stick. Semantic transfer or shift may also occur in borrowing. For example, a borrowed form, *manshon*, which comes from English "mansion," is used to mean a condominium (in no sense a huge house with a big garden). Pseudo-borrowings using *katakana* appear to involve similar types of semantic transfers, shifts, and narrowings. Observe the following example.

8. Hara   no   deta   *ojisan*
   stomach   GEN   sticked out   middle-aged man
   a *middle-aged man* with his thickening waist

This sentence appears in the advertisement section of a weekly magazine for a diet program. The word *ojisan* (middle-aged man) is used to describe not just a middle-aged man but a person who has lost his sharp appearance and is not young any more. In other words, in this context, *ojisan* is a person whose physical appearance is deteriorating. One reason why the writer chose to write *ojisan* as a pseudo-borrowing seems to lie in the function of borrowing—rendering an entity as something modern or fashionable. In other words, by using *katakana*, the writer avoids making the already undesirable person more undesirable. It is possible to hypothesize that the writer reduced *ojisan's* negative connotation by writing it in *katakana*, which is associated with being modern or fashionable. Another possible interpretation is that the pseudo-borrowing adds a sense of casualness or informality to the sentence, which in turn helps reduce the seriousness of the negative image of a middle-aged man.

This line of analysis suggests that borrowing may serve as a politeness strategy perhaps resembling a tactic discussed by Brown and Levinson (1987). Pseudo-borrowing, as well as traditional borrowing, can function as a discourse strategy to avoid face-threatening situations.

Pseudo-borrowing and Politeness

According to Brown and Levinson (1987), a rational speaker will try to save face in cooperative interaction. The researchers proposed two types of "face." Positive face seeks the preservation of positive self-image. It reflects the human desire to be appreciated and approved of by others. Negative face is the desire that one's actions should not be impeded by others. It is argued that people use various face-saving politeness strategies to avoid threatening either face or both faces. For example, disagreement is an intrinsically face-threatening act because it usually indicates that the addressee's opinion is not approved or appreciated by the speaker (or vice versa), thus threatening the addressee's positive face. Requests are another type of potentially face-threatening act because there may be an imposition of the speaker's wants on the addressee, thus threatening the addressee's negative face.

The use of pseudo-borrowing can be accounted for within the framework of politeness strategy. In (8), we observed the use of the pseudo-borrowing *ojisan*. The writer of (8) was probably addressing the average middle-aged man whose physical appearance is decaying and who is feeling miserable or frustrated by getting old. Thus, by describing a typical middle-aged man through a pseudo-borrowing, the writer found a way to mitigate any possible threat to an addressee's positive face (i.e., positive self-image). Pseudo-borrowing is an effective tool for this purpose. The writer can add a positive tone to the word *ojisan*, thereby taking advantage of the generally positive meaning associated with borrowings. Alternatively, it is possible that, through the use of *katakana*, which was originally reserved for foreign words, the writer seeks to be distant or indirect, by attaching a sense of remoteness (being foreign) to the word *ojisan*. This could be characterized as an "off record" politeness strategy, in which "the actor cannot be held to have committed himself to one particular intent" (Brown and Levinson 1987:69). In any case, by using *katakana* the writer is avoiding any commitment to a negative connotation of the word meaning "a middle-aged man."

Similarly, observe the following example.

9. Otoko   ni-totte-no   *konpurekkusu*   to   ie-ba   *hage*
    male   for   inferiority complex   COMP   if we say bald
    If we name an *inferiority complex* for males, it is being *bald*.

The word *konpurekkusu* 'inferiority complex' is a borrowing from English and it is written in *katakana*. This is no surprise, given the function of *katakana*. However, interestingly enough, the Japanese word *hage* 'bald', which is not a foreign word, is also written in *katakana*. The underlying motivation for writing *hage* in *katakana* can also be attributed to a politeness strategy, as in (8). Given that being bald is not desirable for males, writing *hage* in *hiragana* or *kanji* would be a threat to an addressee's positive face. A way to mitigate this threat is to treat the word as if it were foreign by writing it in *katakana*. In other words, pseudo-borrowing is a way to protect the face of the addressee (reader).

Here is an example taken from a short story in a weekly magazine.

10. Ore   *batsu*   *ichi*   ya   kra   na
     I   wrong mark/punishment   one   TAG   because   TAG
     I have *divorced once*, you know.

In (10), the Japanese word *batsu ichi* 'once-divorced person' is written in *katakana* as a pseudo-borrowing. *Katakana* is used to show that *batsu ichi* is a newly created word. It almost seems like a foreign word. It is possible to assume that the writer sought to save his positive face (i.e., the positive self-image) by writing the word in *katakana*. In Japan, divorce is usually viewed negatively: a divorced person is generally considered a failure not only in his or her marriage but in his or her social life. The use of *katakana* for the word *batsu ichi* 'once-divorced person' is a skillful way for the writer to establish a sense of remoteness from the actual referent of the word. In other words, the writer successfully distances himself or herself from the undesirable referent, which in turn leads to the retention of his or her positive face. Pseudo-borrowing, or using *katakana* for nonforeign concepts, is an effective way to mitigate a threat to one's positive face, thus serving as a politeness strategy.

The following example is taken from a magazine article about the U.S. presidential election.

11.

Watashi	ni	toohyoo	sure	ba
I	for	vote	do	if
Hillary	ga	*omake*	ni	tsuitekuru
Hillary	NOM	free gift	as	come

If you vote for me, Hillary comes as a *free gift.*

The sentence was framed as an utterance claimed to have been said by Mr. Clinton. To describe Mrs. Clinton as a free gift is obviously rude. Thus, the writer uses *katakana* for the word, creating a casual and informal tone. By doing so, the writer avoids (or at least pretends to avoid) treating Mrs. Clinton, the first lady of the United States, as an auxiliary object. The pseudo-borrowing is a means of saving Mrs. Clinton's positive face.

Next observe the following example from a weekly magazine.

12.

Kimi	wa	kanojo	to	*kankei*	ga	dekita	no	ka
you	TOP	she	with	relations	NOM	established	COM	Q

Did you have *(sexual) relations* with her?

This sentence is from a short story in which the writer (the speaker) is talking about the addressee's relations with a woman. The Japanese word *kankei* is written in *katakana*. The word can refer to various types of relations from foreign diplomatic relations to sexual relations. From the context in which the sentence appears, it is clear that the word specifically means sexual relations. Directly asking an addressee about his sexual relationships could threaten the face of the addressee. Here again, the choice of *katakana* can be explained as a politeness strategy to save the addressee's positive face (and possibly the writer's as well). By writing the word *kankei* in *katakana*, thus treating it as pseudo-borrowing, the writer can distance himself or herself from a very direct request for potentially embarrassing information.

Consider now the following example, which is taken from a conversation between a mother and her daughter in a magazine.

13. Mother:

Yumi chan,	okaasan	naguttari	shite	gomen	ne
loving	mother	hit	did	sorry	TAG

Yumichan, I am sorry for hitting you.

Daughter:

Iino	yo	okaasan,	aaiuno	wa
no	TAG	mother	that	TOP
ai	no	*muchi*	toka	
love	GEN	whipping	COMP	
itte	ii	koto	ni	
said	good	thing	as	
natteiru	rashii	kara		
is	seem	because		

That's all right, because that appears to be called whipping for love.

The Japanese word *muchi* 'whipping' is written in *katakana*. The word could be written in *hiragana* or *kanji*. It should be pointed out that the *kanji* for *muchi* is difficult for many readers to recognize. It has eighteen strokes, compared to other *kanji* such as *ko* (as in [5]), which has only three strokes. The chance that the *kanji* for *muchi* might not be known by the audience may have led the writer not to use *kanji*. However, it is also possible that the choice is related to the function of *katakana*: describing a foreign word. *Muchi* has a semantic association with being cold-hearted. It can be used to refer to mercilessly forcing an unwilling horse to work hard. The negative connotation of the word can be deemphasized by writing it in *katakana*, as if it were a borrowing from some remote foreign language. Consequently, choosing to render the word as a pseudo-borrowing may mitigate the threat to the mother's positive face.

When taboo words (e.g., sexual terms, curse words, words relating to excretion) are to be used, pseudo-borrowing serves as an effective way to avoid putting the writer's positive self-image in jeopardy. Observe the following examples.

14.   *unchi*   'stool'
      oppai   'breast'
      are   'sexual intercourse'
      asoko   'genitals'
      mono   'genitals'

All of these words could easily be written in *hiragana,* yet they are often written in *katakana* as if they were borrowings from a foreign language. By treating taboo words as borrowings, thus reducing the writer's attachment to the socially undesirable image they have, the writer can effectively save face.

Building and maintaining a writer's positive image through establishing a sense of solidarity with readers can also be viewed as a politeness strategy. Brown and Levinson (1987) point out that the use of in-group identity markers (e.g., address forms, dialect, slang) is an effective way to increase the common ground between a speaker and a listener. Especially in societies like Japan, where various social memberships play a crucial role in linguistic behavior (e.g., honorifics), it is not hard to comprehend the notion of inside (*uchi*) or outside (*soto*) as highly relevant. In this system, language use has the potential to function as a discourse strategy to gain (or lose) group membership (e.g., Makino 1996; Shibatani 1990; Tokunaga 1992). In his study of code-switching among bilinguals, Gumperz (1982:66) states the relationship between code choice and its social meaning as follows: "The tendency is for the ethnically specific, minority language to be regarded as the 'we code' and become associated with in-group and informal activities, and for the majority language to serve as the 'they code' associated with the more formal, stiffer and less personal out-group relations."

This statement concerns code-switching, a behavior in those who are bilingual. However, we may extend the notion of "we code" and "they code" to the issue of pseudo-borrowing among those who use only one language as well. Because *katakana* is associated with foreign words whose image is generally less stiff and less formal than the equivalent words in Japanese (Shibatani 1990), its use increases the tone of informality. If this is truly the case, the use of *katakana* (pseudo-borrowing) can generate the same effect as "we code," the code of the in-group, thus generating a sense of solidarity between a writer and readers. The following examples show that pseudo-borrowings are contributing to the promotion of solidarity as a "we code." The sentences appear as comments about TV programs in a journal targeted to young people. The writer is a young TV personality, and he is using an informal style of directly speaking to his audience of young readers.

15. Koohaku   utagassen   wa   kotoshi   de
    red and white   song contest   TOP   this year   by
    47 kaime   ni   naru   ga
    times   to   become   but
    NHK mo   PR   ga   umai   yo   *na*
    too   advertising   NOM   good   TAG   TAG
    This year will be the 47th red-and-white song contest. NHK [TV station] is still good at promoting the program, *right?*

16. *Ore*   no   bangumi   no   hoo   ga   yoppodo
    I   GEN   program   GEN   side   NOM   far more
    genki   ga   deru   *ze*
    high spirit NOM   come out   TAG
    My (TV) program is far more fun to watch, *right?*

In (15), the Japanese tag *na* 'aren't they' is written in *katakana*. In (16), the pronoun *ore* 'I' and the tag *ze* 'isn't it' are also written in *katakana*. The writer uses pseudo-borrowing as "we code," which is associated with informality and in-group membership with the addressee. By generating a sense of solidarity with the addressee, the writer increases the chances that his comments will be accepted. In other words, the writer was successful in building and maintaining his positive self-image or face. Thus, the pseudo-borrowing can be viewed as a skillful discourse strategy to gain social approval from an addressee.

As a final note, it should be pointed out that it is highly likely that multiple functions are embedded within each pseudo-borrowing. Thus, the analysis for each example in this essay does not exclude other interpretations. Rather, the present analysis has shown that pseudo-borrowing has more functions than merely that of emphasis.

Conclusion

The language contact situation in contemporary Japan has resulted in a large number of both cultural and core borrowings (mainly from English). These borrowings are rendered in Japanese, using the *katakana* writing system, which is traditionally reserved for foreign borrowings. This study suggests that the Japanese have created a new type of borrowing, the pseudo-borrowing. Unlike languages that have only one writing system (such as English), Japanese has three writing systems. One of the writing systems, *katakana*, is generally reserved for borrowings. Now, however, native Japanese words are sometimes written as if they were borrowings. These are what I call pseudo-borrowing.[4] The function of those pseudo-borrowings is similar to that of traditional borrowings: to convey a tone of modernity, internationalism, and sophistication.

This study has also argued that the function of pseudo-borrowings can be extended to issues of politeness. People often look for ways to mitigate the face-threatening potential of speech acts. Brown and Levinson (1987) proposed various politeness strategies for saving face in conversation. I have shown that pseudo-borrowing can function as a politeness strategy in Japanese writing. The results of this study suggest that politeness strategies are not limited to speaking as was originally conceived by Brown and Levinson (1987), but are applicable to writing (orthography) as well.[5]

References

Azuma, S. 1997a. "Borrowing and Politeness Strategy." *Berkeley Linguistics Society* 22:3–12.

———. 1997b. *Shakai Gengogaku Nyuumon* [An introduction to sociolinguistics]. Tokyo: Kenkyuusha.

Brown, P., and Levinson, S. 1987. *Politeness: Some Universals in Language Usage.* Cambridge: Cambridge University Press.

Gumperz, J. 1982. *Discourse Strategies.* Cambridge: Cambridge University Press.

Haarmann, H. 1984. "The Role of Ethnocultural Stereotypes and Foreign Languages in Japanese Commercials." *International Journal of the Sociology of Language* 50:101–21.

---

[4] It would be interesting to examine the phenomenon of pseudo-borrowing diachronically (e.g., when did pseudo-borrowing begin?). Such an examination, however, is beyond the scope of this study.

[5] In his study of code-mixing in Hong Kong newspaper columns, Li (1996) discusses many cases where English words appear in their alphabetic script in a Chinese text as a discourse strategy.

Hayashi, T., and Hayashi, R. 1995. "A Cognitive Study of English Loanwords in Japanese Discourse." *World Englishes* 14(1):55–66.

Honna, N. 1995. "English in Japanese Society: Language within Language." *Journal of Multilingual and Multicultural Development* 16(1 & 2):45–62.

Iwasaki, Y. 1994. "Englishization of Japanese and Acculturation of English to Japanese Culture." *World Englishes* 13(2):261–72.

Kay, G. 1995. "English Loanwords in Japanese." *World Englishes* 14(1):67–76.

Li, D. C. S. 1996. *Issues in Bilingualism and Biculturalism: A Hong Kong Case Study.* New York: Peter Lang.

Loveday, L. 1986. *Explorations in Japanese Sociolinguistics.* Amsterdam: John Benjamins.

———. 1996. *Language Contact in Japan.* Oxford: Clarendon Press.

Makino, S. 1996. *Uchi to Soto no Gengobunkagaku* (Cultural linguistics of "inside" and "outside"). Tokyo: ALC Press.

Miyaji, H. 1990. "June 1987: A Study of *Gairaigo.*" In *On Japanese and How to Teach It,* ed. O. Kamada and W. M. Jacobsen, pp. 15–23. Tokyo: Japan Times.

Morrow, P. 1987. "The Users and Uses of English in Japan." *World Englishes* 6(1):49–62.

Myers-Scotton, C. 1992. "Comparing Code-Switching and Borrowing." In *Codeswitching,* ed. C. M. Eastman, pp. 19–23. Clevedon: Multilingual Matters.

———. 1993. *Social Motivations for Codeswitching: Evidence from Africa.* Oxford: Clarendon Press.

Ono, R. 1992. "Englishized Style Repertoire in Modern Japanese Literature." *World Englishes* 11(1):29–50.

Shibatani, M. 1990. *The Languages of Japan.* Cambridge: Cambridge University Press.

Stanlow, J. 1987. "Japanese and English: Borrowing and Contact." *World Englishes* 6(2):93–109.

Takashi, K. 1990. "A Sociolinguistic Analysis of English Borrowings in Japanese Advertising Texts." *World Englishes* 9(3): 327–41.

Takebe, Y. 1979. *Nihongo no Hyooki* (Writing in Japanese). Tokyo: Kadokawa shoten.

Tokunaga, M. 1992. "Dichotomy in the Structures of Honorifics of Japanese." *Pragmatics* 2(2):124–40.

EIGHT

Language Change: Accents in the Tokyo Dialect

HIROKO STORM

Japanese language of the twentieth century is considerably different from that of the nineteenth century. Likewise, it can be assumed that Japanese language of the twenty–first century will be different from that of the twentieth century.

Changes can be seen in various aspects of the language. Old vocabulary is gone, and new vocabulary appears. Conjugation is changing, too. Here is an example: *rare*, which means "can," is attached to a verb, and the combination means "can—." For example, *taberareru* means "can eat" (*tabe* 'eat', *rare* 'can'; *ru* is present tense). People often delete *ra* and say *tabereru*. *Mirareru* 'can see' becomes *mireru*. Although *tabereru* and *mireru* are widely used, they are not considered perfectly acceptable. However, it is conceivable that they may become standard forms in the future.

Pronunciation is changing, too. When *g* occurs in the middle of a word, *g* is often nasalized, e.g., *hağaki* 'postcard'. It is said that young people do not nasalize *g* any more. Accent change is occurring, too.[1] In this chapter, I will show that accent change. More specifically, I will show that the number of unaccented words is increasing. The definition of "unaccented" will be

---

[1] For more language change phenomena, see "Sugata Kaeyuku Nihongo" (Changing Japanese), *Nihon Keizai Shinbun*, Nov. 23, 1998. This is a symposium by several scholars and writers. According to a survey by Nippon Hoso Kyokai (NHK), 84 percent of the people regard the Japanese language change phenomena as *midare* 'corruption'. However, some speakers point out that language change should not be regarded as *midare*. I agree that *midare* is not a pertinent term to describe language change. Language is dynamic, and language change is a normal aspect of language.

shown below. I will then extend the discussion to Japanese
language education in terms of accent for nonnative speakers.

This chapter focuses on accent change in the Tokyo dialect. In
the nineteenth century, the Japanese government designated the
Tokyo dialect as standard Japanese. Thus, the Tokyo dialect is
basically the same as standard Japanese. Before proceeding to the
main part of the chapter, I will briefly note mechanisms of
Japanese accents.

Japanese accents words through pitch, while English does so
through stress. For example, in English, the word *electricity* has an
accent on *ri*, which is pronounced with stress—*electrícity*. In contrast, in Japanese, each *mora*, which is similar to a syllable, has a
high pitch or a low pitch.[2] Each dialect has its own pitch patterns.
The following are two characteristics of pitch patterns in the
Tokyo dialect. (1) If the first mora is high-pitched, the second
mora is always low-pitched, and if the first mora is low-pitched,
the second mora is always high-pitched. (2) High-pitched moras
can never be interrupted by a low-pitched mora or low-pitched
moras. The patterns in (a), for example, are acceptable, but the
patterns in (b) are not:

(H = high	L = low)		
(a)	LHHHL	HLLLL	LHLLLLL
(b)	LHHLH	HLHLL	LHLHHHH

The locus of the accent in a word is where the pitch drops, as
the following examples show: (1) LHLLL (*o-ka-a-sa-n* 'mother'); the
mora *ka* is accented. LHHLLL (*to-o-mo-ro-ko-shi* 'corn'); the mora
mo is accented. Consider the following: (1) HL (*ha-shi* 'chopsticks'); (2) LH (*ha-shi* 'bridge'); (3) LH (*ha-shi* 'edge'). In the word
for "chopsticks," *ha* is accented. In contrast, the words for
"bridge" and "edge" look the same. That is, in both of the words,
ha is low-pitched, and *shi* is high-pitched. However, when you
use a particle such as *mo* 'also' after the words, an accentual
difference shows up: (1) LHL (*ha-shi mo* 'bridge also'); (2) LHH
(*ha-shi mo* 'edge also'). The word for "bridge" has an accent on
shi, where a pitch fall occurs toward the particle. In the case of
the word for "edge," no pitch fall occurs. Words where no pitch

---

[2] For Japanese accents in general, see Timothy Vance, *An Introduction to Japanese
Phonology* (New York: State University of New York Press, 1987); and Tsujimura
Natsuko, *An Introduction to Japanese Linguistics* (Cambridge: Blackwell, 1996).

fall occurs are called "unaccented words." Here are some more examples of unaccented words: (1) LHHHH (*ga-ku-se-i mo* 'student also'); (2) LHHH (*ko-do-mo mo* 'child also'); (3) LHHHHH (*o-mo-i-ya-ri mo* 'sympathy also').

Inoue reports that there is a recent tendency for borrowed words used in Japanese industry to be deaccented. He also briefly mentions that it has been noted that among borrowed words in general, too, deaccentuation has been noticed since the end of the 1970s.[3]

Recently, I have felt that the number of unaccented words is increasing, whether they are borrowed or nonborrowed.[4] That is, Japanese vocabulary as a whole is losing accent. I have heard other people saying the same thing. So I tried to see whether it is really happening by conducting some tests.

Application of Pronunciation Tests

I conducted three kinds of tests in 1998. Informants were all in their twenties, and from Tokyo or near Tokyo. The data used for the tests are limited to nouns.

For the first test, I picked up words at random from an accent dictionary published in 1974.[5] I picked up 60 two-mora words, 60 three-mora words, 60 four-mora words, and 40 five-mora words—a total of 220 words.

Because words in isolation cannot show correct accentuation (as in the case of *hashi* 'bridge' and *hashi* 'edge', mentioned earlier), I made a simple sentence using each word. In making sentences, I considered two things.

First, the pitch pattern of a word is often influenced by the preceding word. For example, the pitch pattern of *sora* 'sky' is HL, but when it is preceded by *aoi* 'blue', the pitch pattern of *sora*

---

[3] Inoue Fumio, "Gyokaigo no Akusento: Senmonka Akusento no Seikaku" (Accents on industry vocabulary: Characteristics of accents used by professionals). *Gengo* 21.2 (1992): 34–39. In Nishio Hiroko, "Accent of English Borrowed Words in the Osaka Dialect of Japanese" (M.A. thesis, California State University, Fresno, 1975), I examined accents of borrowed words in the Tokyo and Osaka dialects. I noticed deaccentuation to some extent, but it was not so conspicuous yet.

[4] Japanese vocabulary consists of three kinds of words—native, Sino-Japanese (Chinese origin introduced many centuries ago), and borrowed (foreign origin except Sino-Japanese). Here, "nonborrowed" means native or Sino-Japanese.

[5] Nippon Hoso Kyokai (NHK), ed., *Nihongo Hatsuon Akusento Jiten* (The Japanese pronunciation and accent dictionary) (Tokyo: Nippon Hoso Shuppan Kyokai, 1974).

becomes LL. Therefore, I used each word at the beginning of a sentence. Second, I avoided the particle *no* 'of' after the word. *No* influences the accentuation of the preceding word. For example, *hashi* 'bridge' has an accent on *shi* as shown before. When *no* is attached, the accent on *shi* disappears. Thus, in the phrase *hashi no ue* 'top of the bridge', the pronunciation is LHH (*ha-shi no*). That is, no pitch fall occurs after *shi*. In other words, the accent disappears.

Each informant was asked to read the 220 sentences. The sequences were randomly ordered with regard to the number of moras. There were fourteen informants. The result of the test shows that some unaccented words are changing into accented words, and some accented words are losing accents.

	unaccented		accented
2-mora words		→	2 words
		←	7 words
3-mora words		→	3 words
		←	13 words
4-mora words		→	1 word
		←	7 words
5-mora words		→	1 word
		←	1 word

Except for five-mora words, deaccentuation is occurring.[6]

For the second test, I made up nonsense words—5 two-mora words, 5 three-mora words, 5 four-mora words, 5 five-mora words, and 5 six-mora words. Totally there were twenty-five nonsense words. Each sentence with a nonsense word had the pattern ＿＿＿ *ga imasu* 'There is a ＿＿＿.' I asked the informants to imagine these nonsense words are names of animals.[7] There were nine informants. Since there were five words of each length, altogether there were forty-five utterances of each length. The result is as follows: In two-mora words, the first mora is usually accented.

---

[6] Here are some sample sentences with words that are losing accents:

Mei ga kita. "My niece came." All the informants pronounced *mei* 'niece' without an accent.

Hakari de hakatta. "I weighed it with a scale." Five informants pronounced *hakari* 'scale' without an accent.

Hoshiebi o tabeta. "I ate dried shrimp." Eight informants pronounced *hoshiebi* 'dried shrimp' without an accent.

[7] Here are some of the samples: *Kuya ga imasu. Mirura ga imasu. Tamimare ga imasu. Tosakuriga ga imasu. Migunamasara ga imasu.*

Only four utterances (9 percent) were unaccented. In three-mora words, twenty-three utterances (51 percent) were accented, twenty-two utterances (49 percent) were unaccented. In four-mora words, 100 percent were unaccented. In five-mora words, six utterances (13 percent) were unaccented. In six-mora words, eight utterances (18 percent) were unaccented.

In the accent dictionary that I used for the first test, percentages of unaccented words are as follows: two-mora words, 17 percent; three-mora words, 48 percent; four-mora words, 73 percent; five-mora words, 26 percent; six-mora words, 17 percent. The result of the test with nonsense words roughly corresponds to the percentages of unaccented words in the dictionary. It seems that saying four-mora words without an accent is Tokyo dialect speakers' inherent tendency. One can speculate that four-mora words are the most susceptible to losing accents over time.

In the third test, I examined the accent pattern of the vocabulary that Teikyo Loretto Heights University students from Japan created. It is often the case that students in a school create their own vocabulary, which outsiders do not understand. For example, *omotekin* is a combination of *omote* 'front' and *kin* 'King Soopers' (a grocery store chain in Colorado). The word means "King Soopers on the front side of Teikyo Loretto Heights University," as opposed to *urakin* 'King Soopers on the back side of Teikyo Loretto Heights University' (*ura* 'back'). I collected forty-seven words. Twelve informants were asked to read sentences with the words.[8]

Thirty-four words were pronounced without an accent by all the informants. Seven words were pronounced without an accent by some (sometimes a majority) of the informants. Among the forty-seven words, thirty-six words are four-mora words, so it can be assumed that the predominance of four-mora words accounts for the predominance of unaccented words.

Female teenagers in Japan have created their own vocabulary: *kogyarugo* (*ko* 'small, young', *gyaru* 'gal', *go* 'language, word').[9] *Kogyarugo* words also appear to be similar to the vocabulary used

---

[8] Besides *omotekin* and *urakin*, some of the samples are *Ameshoku o tabeta* 'I ate American food' (*ameshoku* 'American food'). *Ofukyan ni sunda* 'I lived off-campus' (*ofukyan* 'off-campus'). *Korosupu ni itta* 'I went to Colorado Springs' (*korosupu* 'Colorado Springs').

[9] Basic data came from *Gendaiyogo no Chishiki* (Knowledge of modern vocabulary) (Tokyo: Jiyukokuminsha, 1998), 1184–87; and Koyama Kohei, "Kogyarugo ni tsuite" (On *Kogyarugo*) (manuscript, 1997).

in Teikyo Loretto Heights University. That is, the majority of the words are four-mora words, and unaccented.[10]

It seems that a word with four moras is the most comfortable length for new creations. Among new words created after the 1940s are many four-mora words. Out of 175 words that I collected, 115 words (66 percent) are four-mora words.[11] The more four-mora words, the more unaccented words. To summarize, as we have seen in test 1, already existing two-, three-, and four-mora words are losing accents. In addition, newly created words tend to be four-mora words, and four-mora words tend to be pronounced without being accented. It appears that Japanese is moving toward deaccentuation as far as nouns are concerned.

Accents in Japanese Language Education

I am also considering how Japanese accents can be incorporated into Japanese language education for nonnative speakers of Japanese. I compared native speakers' Japanese and English speakers' Japanese in terms of accents, using NHK announcers' Japanese as data of native speakers' Japanese, while collecting data of English speakers' Japanese from various sources on TV and in person. During approximately one hour of talk by NHK announcers, 55 percent of the nouns were unaccented. During nearly one hour of talking in Japanese by English speakers, only 21 percent of the nouns were unaccented.[12] In spite of the tendency for the number of unaccented words to increase over time, nonnative speakers' Japanese has many fewer unaccented words.

I also asked two English speakers who have been studying Japanese for some years to do the previously mentioned test with nonsense words that I had conducted with native speakers. Their utterances of nonsense words were all accented. This is not surprising inasmuch as in English, every word has an accent. English speakers inherently tend to put accents somewhere in words when they speak Japanese.

---

[10] I checked accents of *kogyarugo* with an informant.

[11] Basic data came from two books that describe new words: Ishiwata Toshio, "Gendai no Goi" (The modern vocabulary), in *Koza Kokugoshi* (A symposium on the history of Japanese), vol. 3 (Tokyo: Taishukan Shoten, 1973), 345–411; Kamo Shoichi, *Shingo no Kosatsu* (The study of new words) (Tokyo: Sanseido, 1944).

[12] I did not include compound nouns in the number, only single nouns. Words that were used more than one time were counted only once.

I realize that Japanese language teachers (including me) have neglected teaching accents because incorrect accentuation rarely hampers communication. For example, let's consider the three cases of *hashi* again.

	Tokyo	Osaka
	H L	L H
chopsticks	*ha–shi*	*ha–shi*
	L H	H L
bridge	*ha–shi*	*ha–shi*
	L H	H H
edge	*ha–shi*	*ha–shi*

We can see that the pitch patterns of the Osaka dialect differ from those of the Tokyo dialect. However, Tokyo dialect speakers and Osaka dialect speakers can communicate with each other almost perfectly.

In my instruction of Japanese, after explaining Japanese accents briefly at the beginning, I try not to be meticulous about students' accents. There are other important things students have to struggle to learn, such as complicated grammar and complicated *kanji* characters. So if I were too concerned about students' accents, they would get discouraged. In addition, research on accent instruction is very limited, too.[13]

To conclude, I think we can safely say (1) that the number of unaccented words is increasing in Japanese and (2) that English speakers tend to put an accent in a word when they speak Japanese.

Then, it is plausible to say that the gap between native speakers' Japanese and English speakers' Japanese is widening in terms of accents. If they are to conform to the trends regarding

---

[13] To my knowledge, only the following two articles deal with accents in the scope of Japanese language instruction: Horiguchi Junko, "Eigokokumin ni yoru Nihongo no Shionsetsumeishi no Akusento no Yosoku to Sono Jissai" (The "educated guess" in the accent patterns of Japanese four-mora nouns by English-speaking students), *Nihongo Kyoiku* 19 (1973): 97–112. This article discusses how English speakers pronounce four-mora nouns. Accentuation differs according to the syllable structure of the word (e.g., CVCVCVCV, CVVCVCV, etc.). The author predicts the loci of accents, and compares her prediction and the result of tests where informants utter words.

Ayuzawa Takako, "Nihongo Gakushusha ni totte no Tokyogo Akusento" (Accents of the Tokyo dialect for Japanese-language students), *Gengo* 27.1 (1998): 70–75. This article examines how native and foreign language speakers perceive loci of accents. Perception differs, depending on the informant's native language.

accentuation, English speakers may need better guidance when they learn Japanese. For a better pedagogical approach in the twenty-first century, accent instruction is worth exploring. In this chapter, I have discussed only nouns. Other parts of speech, such as verbs and adjectives, are beyond the scope of this study, but they would be worth examining, too.